US-Iran Relations in
Clinton's Second Term:
International Perspectives

Proceedings of the Fourth Conference on US-Iran Relations
April 25, 1997, Washington, D.C.

ISBN   0-9651596-1-2

US-Iran Relations in Clinton's Second Term: International
Perspectives
Edited by Hooshang Amirahmadi

Printed in the United States of America

The American-Iranian Council, Inc.

The American-Iranian Council, Inc. is the successor to U.S.-Iran Conference, Inc., a non-profit educational organization founded in 1992 by Professor Hooshang Amirahmadi, Director of Middle Eastern Studies at Rutgers University, New Brunswick. The mission of the AIC is to promote, through the free exchange of ideas, sustained dialogue and a comprehensive understanding between the peoples and governments of the United States and Iran, with the goal of promoting cooperation and enhancing relations between the two nations.

In striving towards this mission, the AIC undertakes original research and analysis, and organizes meetings of eminent academicians, policy experts, government officials, corporate executives, and community leaders to discuss strategic issues in U.S.-Iran relations. The conference summarized in this publication marks the fourth such major event held in Washington, D.C. Proceedings of the previous conferences are available upon request. They include: *The Clinton Administration and the Future of US-Iran Relations; U.S.-Iran Relations: Areas of Tension and Mutual Interest;* and *Revisiting Iran's Strategic Significance in the Emerging Regional Order.* For information, please write to: The American-Iranian Council, Inc., 20 Nassau Street, Suite 512, Princeton, NJ 08542. USA. Phone: (609) 252-9099. Fax: (609) 252-9565.

US-Iran Relations in Clinton's Second Term: International Perspectives

Preface:

This conference was jointly produced by the American-Iranian Council, Inc., Princeton, New Jersey, and the Middle East Institute, Washington, D.C. The event was supported by the Middle Eastern Studies Program of Rutgers University, New Brunswick, New Jersey. Special appreciation is extended to the sponsors, Conoco Corporation and the Center for World Dialogue, as well as to many who attended, including corporate executives, government officials, academicians, policy and legal experts, and journalists.

The conference was taped and the transcript was made available to the speakers for editing their respective contributions. Anthony Cordesman, Center for Strategic and International Studies, and Steven Rosen, American-Israeli Public Affairs Committee, did not wish their presentations included in this volume. They spoke at the panel on "American Perspectives."

We are grateful to the colleagues who took time to edit their contributions and turn them in on time for publications. Most speakers did not provide a title for their presentations. For uniformity and better readability, I took the liberty of providing titles for them. As the readers can judge for themselves, the speeches are rich and make significant contributions to our understanding of the issues that stand between the two nations.

Many helped in organizing the conference. Special thanks are due to Ambassador Roscoe Suddarth and Andrew Parasiliti of the Middle East Institute, Ali Mafinezam of Rutgers University, and Alyia Rab of the Caspian Associates, Inc.

In editing this volume, I have benefited from the advice and editorial assistance of a few very fine colleagues. Among them, Janice Moore Zangeneh deserves special mention and my sincere appreciation. Needless to say that I, as editor, remain accountable for any editorial mistakes or shortcomings.

The AIC is an open forum for exchange of diverse perspectives as reflected in this publication. As such it does not take side in the debates and is not accountable for views expressed by the contributors.

This conference was organized in the wake of the Mykonos verdict against the Islamic Republic of Iran. Thus, the environment within which the event took place was tense to say the least. Nevertheless, the free market place of ideas in the United States made it possible for the participants to engage in a lively debate as is reflected in the following pages.

Now, only a few months later, a more hospitable environment has emerged in the Unted States concerning Iran following the May 1997 presidential election there. President Mohammad Khatami's belief in dialogue among civilizations has led him to open up a "dialogue" with "the great American people," and "the great American civilization." Reciprocating these positive expressions, President Bill Clinton has also recognized Iranians as "a great people" and spoken of their civilization with sincere admiration.

This is of course a gratifying development for some of us who have advocated a better understanding and improved relations between the two nations. We can only be hopeful that the current desire for a people-to-people diplomacy or cultural exchanges will soon develop into a more serious dialogue between the two governments for building mutual trust and enhanced relations between the two nations.

Hooshang Amirahmadi
February 1998

Table of Contents

Welcoming Remarks

Roscoe Suddarth
President, The Middle East Institute

Thank you for coming. I am Roscoe Suddarth, President of the Middle East Institute. I would like to welcome you all here today to talk about US-Iran relations during President Clinton's second term.

I would like to start by thanking our cosponsor from Rutgers University, Dr. Hooshang Amirahmadi, his colleague, Mr. Ali Mafinezam, and certainly the folks at the Middle East Institute who worked so hard to put this conference together — Mr. Andrew Parasiliti, the Director of Programs, Middle East Institute, Mr. Mohammed Khraishah, also of the Middle East Institute, and our excellent interns.

Let me just say a word to start things off. Over the past few months, and especially after having participated in a couple of study groups focusing upon Iran, I have been struck by a disparity between two aspects of Iran's international relationships. On one hand are the really dismal, current prospects for improvement in relations between the United States and Iran. These prospects are balanced, on the other hand, against the strategic importance that accompanies the establishment of a long term, positive relationship between the two countries. On an even broader scale, I am struck by the dim prospects for improved relations between Iran and most of the Western community, even though, in the long run, the strategic importance of a positive relationship between Iran and the West is indisputable.

In the immediate present, our attention is focused upon the Mykonos trial and its effects; the Al Khobar bombing and the question of whether or not Iran was involved; and in particular, the Iranian elections which will take place in May, 1997. As you know, the prospects are for Nateq Nuri, the hard-line Speaker of the Parliament to succeed President Rafsanjani.

Meanwhile, as someone put it rather cogently, there is no political gain for either the President of the United States or officials within Iran to work to improve US-Iranian relations. If steps were taken to improve relations, this would fuel the criticism of political groups standing in opposition to Clinton, as well as of groups in Iran who oppose leaders who might favor the development of a dialogue.

Given these factors it appears that, in the short run, things are probably going to get worse before they get better in regard to Iran's relationship with the United States and Western Europe. However, concern about the need for a long-term strategic relationship with Iran has been evidenced on the part of the policy community in the West. It is my hope that both the short and long-term issues impacting upon the relationship between these two countries will be clarified during this conference. The significance of this undertaking may be illuminated by questions such as the following:

- How can a population that is supposed to grow to 105 million by the year 2015 be ignored by the world community?
- How can a country with the second-largest petroleum reserves in the world [sic] and the longest coastline in the Persian Gulf be ignored?
- How do we ignore the strategic effects of the pipeline issue, in terms of Central Asian independence from Russia over the longer term, and the effects on Turkey, an ally of the U.S.?
- How do we ignore the effects of the prolonged period of tension upon our allies in the Gulf and upon U.S. business as it loses out?
- And, as with Iraq, how does one rationalize the continued constraints on oil and gas production with the prospect that Asian economic growth will lead to increased demand for additional Gulf oil and gas supplies?

Let me conclude by saying that I hope the conference will update us on the current situation in Iran. In the absence of the U.S. presence there, it has become increasingly difficult to determine what is really going in Iran. Secondly, I hope this conference will leave us with a better sense of the policy options which might present themselves in the near future, and perhaps, in a more important sense, of those which might emerge over the long run.

I would now like to turn the floor over to our colleague, Dr. Hooshang Amirahmadi, who is well known to many of you as one who keeps the subject of Iran alive in a town where it tends to be taken for granted.

Introductory Remarks

Hooshang Amirahmadi
Professor and Director, Middle Eastern Studies
Rutgers University

Good morning and welcome. Let me begin by thanking Ambassador Roscoe Suddarth and Mr. Andrew Parasiliti, both of the Middle East Institute and respected colleagues, and Ms. Aliya Rab of Caspian Associates, for their help in organizing this conference. In particular, I acknowledge Mr. Ali Mafinezam of Rutgers University for his tenacity and support. He has been instrumental in organizing and publicizing this event. I also want to thank the distinguished speakers who have accepted our invitation to share their thoughts on Iran with an equally distinguished audience. Finally, the sponsorship provided by Conoco, Center for World Dialogue, and the corporate registrants is greatly appreciated.

In the audience today we have many eminent members of the diplomatic community as well as U.S. officials from the Departments of State and Defense, the Office of Management and Budget, and the United States Information Agency. Also, we have a number of influential corporate executives and community leaders, distinguished academicians, well-known journalists, and high level policy and legal experts.

The fact that Iran is a taboo subject, particularly now that the Mykonos verdict is in, means that putting together a forum like this requires much perseverance and vision. It also requires a deep commitment to the idea that the freer and more open the marketplace of ideas in this country becomes, the more successful America will be in the next century.

Thus, I am proud to report that this is the only public forum I know of that brings so many diverse international perspectives to the Iran debate. That these conferences have been well received is evident by the fact that they have continued to attract growing numbers of very distinguished conference participants, and have spurred further debate in other arenas around the world. At present, we are participating in the fourth in a series of annual US-Iran Conferences that I have organized with my colleagues. The first was held in January, 1993, at the very outset of Clinton's first term. Since that time, these conferences have spawned meaningful discussion, analysis, and understanding of issues, and have led to policy recommendations that were ahead of their time.

Close to a million Iranian-Americans live in the United States. Their career success and their adaptability to the demands of American life has been exemplary. From nuclear physics to neurosurgery, from Wall Street finance to high-tech entrepreneurship in Silicon Valley, and even extending into the fashion and television industries, our community is making valuable contributions to America's greatness.

Yet, at the same time, however adapted we might be to the demands of life in this country, we cannot bury our Persian identity and past. The void that we see between these two great nations pains us, because we see it as the mirror image of the struggle for identity that we must deal with every day.

I have lived in this country for 22 years. It is undeniable that one key impetus in my life for building bridges between America and Iran has been to reconcile the fragile identity of immigrant life. On a larger scale, continued animosity between the two governments has the potential to drive a wedge between the peoples of the two great nations — 250 million Americans and 65 million Iranians.

The other motivation for building a bridge across this void is my belief that the mutual interests of the United States and Iran far outweigh their differences. The Persian Gulf and Caspian Sea regions contain two-thirds of the world's oil and gas reserves. And because Iran is the only country that connects these two regions, it has every reason to foster stability in its own neighborhood. The need to keep the energy flowing and to maintain stability throughout the whole region constitutes a major common interest of Iran and the United States.

But the region around Iran remains turbulent. To Iran's north, relations between Azerbaijan and Armenia remain volatile. To its west, Kurdish rebellion threatens Iraq and Turkey. To Iran's south, the Persian Gulf monarchies are facing internal dissent on a new scale. To its east, the turbulence in Afghanistan runs the risk of infecting the southern tiers of the former Soviet Union.

If the U.S. and Iran cooperated, their combined ability to bring stability to the Persian Gulf and Caspian Sea regions would be much greater than what they can achieve individually. The economic benefits of cooperation would be equally immense, particularly vis-à-vis the pipeline routes.

Since 1990 I have said and written that the two countries must adopt a long-term pragmatic approach to their relationship; that they must think strategically well into the next century. What we have been saying for seven years is only now beginning to appear in recent issues of *Foreign Affairs, The New York Times, Sixty Minutes*, and other media outlets.

Efforts designed to promote improved US-Iran relations have occurred not only in the United States, but in Iran as well. Our conferences have received wide coverage in the Tehran press. The interviews I have given to the Iranian media and the articles that I have had published in Iran have opened the door to the discussion of a subject that used to be taboo in Tehran: opening the country up to interactions with the United States. Five years ago no one dared speak openly and favorably about the U.S. in Iran. Now, entire magazine issues are dedicated to the subject.

This has not been a risk-free endeavor, however. Last year, factions who oppose the establishment of closer ties between Iran and the U.S. produced a series of Iranian television programs that were harshly critical of my activities. Some hard-line newspapers in Tehran routinely run articles condemning my views. But we have stayed in the field undeterred for we believe in the cause.

During previous trips to Iran, including a two-week stint this past February, I met dozens of top Iranian officials and Majlis deputies, opinion leaders, and heads of tolerated opposition groups, as well as Western diplomats based in Tehran. We often talked, just as we are doing today, about the future of US-Iran relations.

In ways not always apparent to American eyes, a window of opportunity is opening up in Iran. There is an increasingly strong constituency within the Islamic Republic who favor better ties with the United States. If the U.S. were to replace its current policy of containment with a policy of constructive engagement, this would provide a strong boost to the Iranians in favor of improved relations.

Iranís upcoming presidential elections, to be held in May, 1997, present an opportunity for a new beginning in Iran — a new beginning for domestic reform and for greater integration within the community of nations. The new Iranian President will be in a unique position to help lead the country away from the legacy of the past, and to introduce a new era in the history of the Islamic Republic. The United States must position itself to capitalize upon this opportunity.

For those of us involved in building bridges between the two countries, this opportunity brings new challenges. We intend to be just as innovative as we have been for the past few years. The road ahead involves a recognition in Tehran that the US, as a great political, military, and technological power, will continue to play a central role in the region that surrounds Iran. In Washington, there is the recognition that Iran is destined to be the main regional power in the Caspian Sea-Persian Gulf region, and that, in terms of the geopolitics of energy, Iran is the most strategically significant country in the world.

This mutual recognition must be based on the proposition that power is not a zero-sum game between Iran and the United States. A win-win perspective must come to inform policy making in both countries. As Ruhi Ramazani has said, Iranian and American leaders must put themselves in each others' shoes.

But how can we facilitate that process from our world of ideas? How can we expand knowledge and foster mutual understanding between the two countries? We have already been doing that for some time, through this series of conferences and through writing and publishing. But the time has come to build on our resources, and to institutionalize our activities so that they become more sustainable and effective. Events designed to stimulate intercultural dialogue, such as today's conference, are needed on a more frequent basis. I am thus proposing to build an organization to be known as the iAmerican-Iranian Councilî, AIC, which reflects a culmination of the ideas that have emerged over the past few years, and whose time has come.

Two weeks ago at a conference here in Washington, Bob Pelletreau, in his first appearance after retiring as the Assistant Secretary of State for the Near East, suggested that the way to keep the ball rolling now is through building bridges between the institutions of civil society and the private sector in both countries. That is exactly what we intend to do. In order to fulfill our mission at the AIC, we intend to produce and publish expert and objective analyses of regional geopolitics and strategic issues, bring together interested parties to discuss US-Iran relations from diverse and comprehensive perspectives, and make public, via various media, the insights gained through these and other educational programs.

I am pleased that the American-Iranian Council already has gained the support of distinguished members of think tanks, universities, and the private sector, who have joined the Council in an advisory or executive capacity. But we also need support from charitable foundations and corporations. We will soon communicate further with you about the American Iranian Council, and will ask you all to help us build an effective organization. I am sure that the Council will come to personify the voice of the future on US-Iran relations.

Let me leave you with a final thought. The future of relations between Americans and Iranians is too grand a topic to be viewed strictly through the lens of the Clinton Administration, the 105th Congress, or the leaders of the Islamic Republic. Long after the current political players have left the scene, there still will be two great nations who must one day mend their fences and make the world a better place for posterity. I hope you will join us in furthering this noble cause. Thank you.

PANEL I: AMERICAN PERSPECTIVES

Opening Remarks

Henry Precht (Panel Chair)
Former Country Director for Iran, State Department

Good morning. I am Henry Precht, Chair of this panel. I will provide only brief introductions of myself and the other panelists, as more detailed background information may be found in your folders.

I served in Iran from 1972 to 1976, and was Country Director for Iran in the United States State Department from 1978 to 1980, that is, during the Iranian Revolution and the Hostage Crisis.

Even more succinctly (as I have been introduced in the past), I lost Iran. Not only did I lose it once, I lost it twice in one year; something of a record for a State Department officer, I would say.

In retrospect, one of the curious things that happened during the turmoil of the Hostage period was that, after our embassy was seized and our staff taken prisoner, the United States waited five months before breaking relations with Iran. Now, some of you scholars of government will say that such a delay illustrates the force of inertia in American foreign policy. There was some of that, but another factor was a sort of wishful hopefulness that things would get better, that the Hostage Crisis would be forgotten, and we could pick up and resume a normal relationship, as we had in the past.

These explanations are both valid, but the real reason we did not break relations quickly was that we had the model of China in front of us. We knew that if relations were severed it would be extremely difficult to knit them together again. So it was with great reluctance that the U.S. took that step, 17 years ago this month. We now have four or five years before we catch up with the Chinese model that we feared. From all prospects it seems to me that we will use up all of that time, just as we feared 17 years ago.

When I was living in exile in Cleveland, Ohio, I had an opportunity to talk with the then Chinese Ambassador, who was one of those who helped Dr. Kissinger to reestablish relations with the United States. Having Iran in mind, I asked him what were the crucial factors that enabled the two countries to come together again. He said, "We shared a strategic interest, and we had mutual respect." That is, the U.S. and China were both worried about the Soviet Union, but there was also the important quality of understanding and respect.

Perhaps this panel will identify some shared concerns or interests between Iran and the United States. It will be an exceptional panel indeed if it can divine any mutual respect that exists between our two countries. We shall see.

We begin this conference with an excellent panel. I commend the organizers for having put together such a group of true experts. I will introduce them now, then they will proceed. Questions will be entertained after all the panelists have spoken.

On my right is Dr. Gary Sick, who will kick off. I first knew Dr. Sick when he was Assistant Naval Attaché in Cairo. From there, he moved on, to become National Security Aide to Presidents Ford, Carter, and Reagan. Dr. Sick wrote perhaps the most complete story of the Iranian Revolution and Hostage Crisis in his book, *All Fall Down*. He now teaches at Columbia University as an Adjunct Professor, and is involved in Gulf 2000, with which I am sure many of you are familiar.

Dr. Sick will be followed by Mr. Steven Rosen. Since 1982, Mr. Rosen has been with the American-Israeli Public Affairs Committee, AIPAC, in the capacity of Foreign Issues Chief. Previously he taught at Brandeis University, the Australian National University, and the University of Pittsburgh, and worked with the RAND Corporation.

Dr. John Lichtblau, on my left, is certainly one of the country's leading petroleum experts. He has his own consulting business, and I am sure many of you are familiar with his work.

Unfortunately, one of our scheduled panel discussants, Dr. Michael Vandusen, is unable to be with us this morning. In his place is Dr. Anthony Cordesman. I first knew Dr. Cordesman when he came to our Embassy in Iran in 1972 to bring order and rationality to the Iranian purchases of military equipment. He was an advisor to General Toufanian at the time. His great success in that endeavor led him into a job as a defense expert on the Middle East. Dr. Cordesman has written extensively, and published frequently. He teaches now at Georgetown University, and is associated with the Center for Strategic and International Studies.

Having dispensed with the introductions, we may now get underway, beginning with Dr. Gary Sick.

Changing Iran and Wrong Policies

Gary Sick
Director, Gulf 2000 Project, Columbia, University

Thank you, Mr. Precht. It is a real pleasure to be here this morning, among this very distinguished group and so many old friends.

First of all, I wanted to thank Dr. Hooshang Amirahmadi for arranging these series of meetings, which have really been exceptional. He is doing an extraordinary amount of work that is, in many ways, thankless, and we should all be appreciative of his efforts.

Let me begin by simply telling a story, which I think may be interesting to some of you. Once upon a time there was a world superpower which was, in fact, the sole superpower in the world, having recently defeated its arch-enemy. Also in those days, there was a recent revolutionary power, which had, in fact, broken away from a close relationship with the superpower. This break occurred under humiliating circumstances, which had never been forgiven.

The revolutionary power was in a mess. Its economy had not recovered from the revolution; the country could not pay its bills and its treasury was nearly broke. The leadership of the revolutionary power was faltering at the time. The beloved charismatic leader, who had been a rallying force of the revolution, was now dead, and his followers lacked his touch. Factionalism was rife. There was no agreement at all about the direction that the country should take or about what its foreign policy should be. In fact, it was so bad that some factions even threatened to break away. Popular support was waning. The revolution was no longer what it had been, and the enthusiasm that the people had once expressed was faltering.

This revolutionary power challenged the superpower with a series of grievances over trade and military operations, but the superpower dismissed these efforts with contempt. There were, in fact, some initial military skirmishes between the two. The revolutionary power, not surprisingly, was no match for the superpower, and its forces scattered in the face of superior technology and training.

Finally, the superpower attacked the capitol city of the revolutionary power, and burned all of the major government buildings. This was undertaken in an effort to show who was boss, and to establish a dominant relationship for the future. But to the superpowerís surprise, instead of pushing the revolutionary power into collapse as anticipated, these actions had the opposite effect. The revolutionary leadership revived and began to be more decisive. Factionalism declined, and the people who had advocated secession now backed their leaders instead. Popular support for the government and against the superpower blossomed and became very strong once more, bringing the revolution back to life. In a final skirmish, the revolutionary power drew the forces of the superpower into a trap and defeated them, decisively.

This is, as some of you may have guessed, a true story. The superpower was Great Britain, the revolutionary power was the United States, and the year was 1812. You may recall that during that time the British defeated Napoleon, their arch-enemy. President Madison was dismissed as ineffectual and certainly not up to the tradition of George Washington, and, at the Battle of New Orleans, the final confrontation, the American troops were led by Andrew Jackson.

Now, I am not recounting these events to make historical comparisons. But I think this story can serve as a kind of cautionary tale for any superpower that finds itself dealing with an irascible revolutionary power. I think the lesson to learn from this little bit of history is that things do not always work out the way they were intended, and that an exclusive focus on short-term issues may cause fundamental interests to be overlooked. This is, in fact, the focus of what I want to talk about this morning.

I cannot talk about fundamental interests, essentially from the United States' perspective, without starting with oil. But the interest is not so much with oil as with energy. In my view, as far as Iran is concerned, oil is a short-term issue. While Iran has significant oil resources, its relative reserves are small, and its fields are old and require massive amounts of gas reinjection to keep going. Gas, however, is another matter. If you believe, as I do, that natural gas is going to be the energy fuel of choice in the 21st century, then Iran becomes more significant.

Iran and Russia have 49 percent of all the natural gas reserves in the world. In the past, this was a problem because the transporting of natural gas required pipelines, a fixed infrastructure that leads from one place to another, and very, very long-term contracts. Liquefied natural gas (or LNG) required huge investments, also required fixed locations on both ends, and offered limited flexibility.

The point that I would like to make about the 21st century is that there is a new technique, a new technology which has already been developed, and which is just waiting now to go into full production. This technology enables the transformation of natural gas into liquid fuels. Specifically, the plants that now exist — in Malaysia, and in South Africa when they were under siege — take natural gas, turn it into a middle distillate, and then transform it into a very pure, non-polluting, highly desirable form, somewhat like diesel fuel. This fuel can be put into a tanker and taken around the world wherever you like.

This new technology is here. It is in place. It is coming. And I think it will be utilized to an ever increasing extent. I think Iran is definitely going to make use of this innovative technology to produce an attractive fuel alternative.

However, Iran is quite late in coming to this. After the revolution the country saw in its future an on-going involvement with oil, a commodity which has always generated much income. However, following the Revolution, Iran had difficulty keeping its fields going, and therefore focused all of its attention in that direction.

Iranians are now beginning to discover, about 10 years too late, that they should have been focusing on gas instead of oil, or that they should have had a dual focus on both gas and oil. But there is no question that Iran has the capacity, certainly, to be a major producer of natural gas.

From a long-term perspective, the U.S. policy of deliberately preventing Iran from gaining access to the benign technology and investment capital needed to develop its gas industry is something that will come back to haunt us later on. The world needs energy, and Iran will be a major supplier. Slowing it down and preventing it from playing that role actually works to our disadvantage in the long run, rather than to our advantage. Our present policy seems to assume that the current surplus is going to last forever.

Central Asia is also a factor. There is no good way to transport the oil and gas around the Caspian Sea. Iran, however, provides a natural route, but presently this avenue is blocked, essentially by U.S. policy. And again, I think this is a good example of "shooting ourselves in the foot". We have even acknowledged it in the sanctions legislation by making special exceptions for swap arrangements from the Caspian Sea in an effort to get around some of the problem. But basically what we are doing is forcing Russia to become the dominant power in the region, and not allowing for alternative possibilities.

Another option, or another fundamental objective, it seems to me, is to try to promote a more secular and more moderate Iran. Iran, in fact, has been changing. We tend to think of that country as it appeared in 1979, 1980, 1981, when the revolution was at its peak. Now, 18 years later, Iran looks very different, as anyone who has actually been there and looked around will attest. It is not the same country, and is actually becoming less clerical in its nature. Although the change has been slow, it can be discerned. For instance, there is an extraordinary difference between the number of clerics in the first Majles and the number who are in the fifth Majles (the present one). The decline in numbers has been massive.

To get a job in Iran, it is no longer enough to say that . . . "I fought in the revolution . . . I was tortured by the Shah . . . and therefore I deserve this job". Now, you must also have some education, and must demonstrate some kind of capability. This was not true 18 years ago, but it is true today.

There has also been a dramatic shift in Iran in the sense that it has put its nationalism ahead of the sort of clerical craziness that dominated in the beginning. Let me just quote Mr. Ezzatollah Sahabi, who is a current presidential candidate, or, at least, is applying to be a presidential candidate. As he announced that he was going to become a candidate for the Presidency, he said, in his opening statement, "Iran is first, and then there is Islam". Eighteen years ago such a statement would have had serious repercussions — you would have been put in jail, at a minimum, and simply drummed out. Now, however, here is a man running for president who puts this in his opening statement. There are many other indications along the way that this is changing, as well.

We may not be all that happy to see Iran become more nationalistic, actually. That is not necessarily a good thing. The other countries in the region had their problems with the Shah, who was perhaps the ultra-nationalist. In fact, now Iran is dusting off many of the Shah's old plans and going back to them, and that may not be altogether a good thing. But it is different than a country dominated entirely by Islamic ideology.

Iran has been pursuing a set of policies in Central Asia which is quite different from those we might expect, given the general impression that we have of Iranian policies elsewhere. There, Iranís policies have been moderate, and quite professional. Iranians have been acting as mediators in the Tajik civil war, in the Afghan dispute, in Nagorno Karabak, and they have dealt with the Russians over Chechnya. In each case, instead of promoting Islamic fundamentalism, they have promoted outcomes that involved compromise, and hopefully reason. That is quite a change from 18 years ago.

Unfortunately, I think that U.S. policies are pushing Iran in the opposite direction. Instead of encouraging them to continue along this path, and even acknowledging the good things that the Iranians have accomplished, we tend to continue demonizing them and pushing them into a corner. As a result, the people who would be our logical allies in Iran tend to be on the defensive, while our opponents in Iran have additional justification for their antagonism.

I will just make one other point in terms of our long-term interests. I think that reducing terrorism and external intervention by Iran is essential, that it is in the long-term interest of the United States, and a goal that we should pursue. However, we must recognize, too, that much of the outrage within the United States says as much about the United States as it does about Iran.

What would you say about a country that:

- seven years ago, went across the border to another country, kidnapped a leader of the opposition and has been holding him without trial or charge for the last seven years — one of the longest-running hostage situations in the Middle East?

- six years ago, set off a car bomb in a neighboring country killing 17 people, and its agents were, in fact, subsequently convicted by the courts of that country?
- five years ago, killed an opposition leader in a foreign country and, in the process of conducting a military operation, also killed his wife and six-year-old son?
- three years ago, kidnapped another opposition leader, who also remains in captivity at the present time, with no charges?
- two years ago, killed an opposition leader in a nearby country by blowing his head off?
- and also in the same year, a few months later, in a European country, shot down one of its opposition leaders in cold blood?

What would you say about a country like that?

Well, if it happens to be Israel, which it is, you do not say very much. If you look at the United States' annual survey of terrorism, you will find it very difficult to find mention of any of those events. That does not excuse a country from carrying out assassinations abroad.

I think Iran is pursuing a policy of terrorism in certain cases, but that this has been declining over time. The question is, how do you best convince the Iranians to maintain that decline, as opposed to pushing them in the opposite direction and turning them into a permanent enemy?

Let me just close by putting in a very brief plug for the Gulf 2000 project that I run, which is dedicated to the idea of building bridges, to finding ways to maintain contacts at a time when contacts are, in fact, very limited and hard to find. It is a slow process. But as we saw in the Cold War with the Russians, it is the kind of process that can, in fact, be useful.

In promoting that kind of a process, I would simply ask you to remember that England, which burned the United States Capitol and the White House during the War of 1812, went on to become the greatest friend and partner of that once revolutionary power, the United States. It is worth thinking about. Thank you.

Oil Industry and U.S.-Iran Relations

John Lichtblau
Chairman, Petroleum Industry Research Foundation

I have been asked to discuss US-Iran relations from the viewpoint of the oil industry. I will therefore address only the economic aspects of the sanctions, not the political rationale and justification for imposing the sanctions.

Let me start with a few facts. At its current production level of about 3.65 million barrels a day, Iran is the fourth-largest oil producer in the world. At its current export level of about 2.6 million barrels, it is the second-largest oil exporter after Saudi Arabia. Iranian oil is needed in the world oil trade. If for any reason Iranian exports became unavailable, world oil prices would soar instantly. This would be particularly true if reduced availability occurred while Iraqi oil export was still limited by the UN Security Council.

Current U.S. policy is not designed to block ongoing Iranian oil exports, although in 1995 this was advocated by a majority of United States legislators. The goal of the current U.S. policy is to curb Iranian oil and gas production gradually, progressively reducing the country's earnings from its principal export commodity.

The first, and, up to now, the principal impact which this policy has had upon the oil industry is that it has forced a major U.S. company, Conoco, to back out of an agreement with Iran to develop one of its major off-shore oil fields. Conoco, as you know, had been awarded the Sirri A and E projects in a competitive bid with other international companies. Iranian officials and independent observers have said the award to Conoco at the time was made not only because of its high professional qualification, but also as a political gesture towards the United States. After Conoco was forced out, the French company, Total, eventually took the Sirri project, which is now well on its way towards commercial production, and is expected to reach its 120,000-barrels-a-day target on schedule.

Who were the winners, who were the losers, in this U.S.

Government-imposed withdrawal of Conoco? The winner, obviously, was the French company; the loser, the U.S. company, which had spent several years and some $15 million to prepare the project. Iran, the U.S. government's target for punishment, has remained largely unaffected by the change, except for a delay of several months which resulted due to switching from one foreign company to another.

Shortly after Conoco's withdrawal, the President issued an Executive Order prohibiting U.S. companies from engaging in any business transactions in or with Iran, which meant, among other things, that they could not purchase any Iranian oil. There had been a prohibition on importing Iranian oil into the U.S. since 1987, but until mid-1995 U.S. companies could trade in Iranian oil abroad or use it in their foreign refineries.

The U.S. Administration wanted other industrial countries to follow suit, just as it had hoped they would in 1987. However, as we are aware, no other country joined the U.S. import embargo on the Iranian oil, either in 1987 or in 1995. Thus, the U.S. is now the only country barring all trade in Iranian oil.

Who gained, who lost, by this action? Here again, U.S. companies lost because their flexibility in trading, exchanging, and refining oil has been curtailed relative to their foreign competitors. Iran, on the other hand, was unaffected by the U.S. restriction, except for a brief transition period. It now exports about as much oil as it can, given its rising domestic demand and recent flat production level. The American oil service and equipment companies also lost out under the Executive Order of 1995. Their actual and potential business loss as a result of the Executive Order has been estimated at about $600 million. Of course, their prospective losses — that is, their foregone future earnings — will continue, while the Executive Order is on, so that they will continue to lose money relative to their foreign competitors, who can supply this equipment. Thus, the Administration's attempt to curtail Iran's oil income through a sanctions policy has been an object lesson of the well-known theory that unilateral sanctions in international trade generally do not work.

The United States Congress, which was more eager to punish Iran for its support of terrorism than the White House, recognized the limitation of unilateral sanctions, and passed the Iran and Libya Sanctions Act of 1996. This Act requires the President to impose a variety of sanctions on foreign companies who invest more than $40 million annually in the oil and gas sector of Iran, and in Libya as well. Later this year, the $40 million annually will be reduced to $20 million.

The Act became law, as you know, on August 5, 1996. I will not go into its details, but again, the question is, who was hurt by it? And is it achieving its intended purpose?

The Sanctions Act exempted Total's Sirri project from any U.S. penalty under its grandfather clause. But it did have some negative effect on new foreign investment in Iran. The Chief Executives of two major foreign oil companies, Royal Dutch Shell and British Petroleum, have publicly stated that they cannot ignore the U.S. Sanctions Act because of their companies' large investments in commercial interests in the United States. Arco had also been interested in one of the off-shore projects, but pulled out when the U.S. sanctions policy was announced.

Despite these setbacks, production from the only area where Iran is seeking foreign participation, the Iranian off-shore, has increased in both 1995 and 1996. Production is expected to increase again this year. At year-end 1996, the off-shore area produced about 550,000 barrels a day, an increase of 200,000 barrels a day in the last two years. The Middle East Economic Survey commented last December that, "The Fact that NIOC (the National Iranian Oil Company) off-shore has been able to increase production so substantially in the face of the U.S. sanctions regime is indeed impressive." Most independent forecasts agree with the projection of one million barrels a day of off-shore production by the year 2000.

Iranian on-shore production, which accounts for nearly 85 percent of Iran's total, has always been developed and operated entirely by NIOC without any foreign participation. Thus, for all practical purposes, most Iranian oil production will not be affected by the U.S. Sanctions Act, since Iran is not seeking and has not sought any foreign participation in its on-shore sector.

On-shore production declined slightly in 1995 and 1996, largely due to delay and neglect of the required substantial gas injection, and measures against encroachment to maintain an increased production of these mature but giant oil fields. However, a large increase in Iran's oil revenue last year compared to what had been budgeted — $19 billion actual versus $16 billion budgeted —

has now brought about some increased investment in these areas. Hence, there appear to be beginning signs of a reversal in the recent decline in on-shore production.

U.S. companies will, of course, be barred from supplying any of the required equipment and technology for this operation. In contrast, foreign companies can supply Iran with needed goods and services with no such risk of U.S. sanctions, since the Sanctions Act only penalizes investment, not trade.

In Iran's off-shore sector, which is the principal source of growth in its oil production, substantial foreign investments will be required to expand production to one million barrels a day by the year 2000. It is quite likely that the United States, through its sanctions policy, will slow these investments by keeping out all U.S. companies and will discourage foreign participation by threatening secondary sanctions. As we have seen, a number of major international companies with substantial U.S. business interests are reluctantly abiding by the U.S. sanctions policy.

However, foreign companies with little or no investment or sales in the U.S. face no such constraint. One example is the Malaysian national oil company, Petronas, which has recently taken a 30-percent share in Total's Sirri project. Several European and Canadian companies with no significant exposure in the U.S. have also shown interest in participating in the Iranian off-shore projects, such as the Balal field.

Without any foreign participation, Iranian crude production rose from 2.3 million barrels a day in 1988, just after the end of the Iran-Iraq War, to about 3.6 million barrels a day in 1993. Since then, it has remained in the range of 3.6 to 3.8-million-barrels a day. I think the upper end of the range is probably very close to Iran's sustainable productive capacity.

With some foreign investment certain in the off-shore sector, Iranian production is likely to grow moderately, despite U.S. sanctions. However, it is likely this growth would occur at a slower rate than if there were no sanctions.

But the country's total energy exports will be boosted significantly — and Dr. Sick referred to this — when the first natural gas exports start by 1999. There are several major gas export projects currently under active consideration. The most advanced is a $20 billion, 22-year Iranian-Turkish project, which is scheduled to begin delivery in 1999.

It is not clear whether the project would fall under the U.S. Sanctions Act, because of its initial contract date and due to the fact that all of Turkey's direct investment in the project would be on Turkish territory. But it is clear that the U.S. does not want Turkey to go through with the project, and has said so adamantly and publicly. Yet, as of now, Turkey seems determined to go ahead. If it does, U.S. firms may well be excluded from participation under current U.S. policy. Thus, here again, the project will be built; the gas will be exported; and the only losers under our policy might be U.S. companies.

Another major gas project is the South Pass off-shore project in which Iran seeks international participation. Currently Total is reported to be the front-runner on this.

Another aspect of Iran's oil industry that could affect U.S. companies is its littoral, or coastal, Caspian Sea location. This was already mentioned. As reported, Iran has backed Russia's claim that all countries bordering on the Caspian must approve any off-shore oil development beyond their territorial coastal zone.

The Caspian Sea may contain ultimate oil reserves in the 40-to-60-billion-barrels range. NIOC is actively exploring its Caspian Sea coastal area, and has a 10-percent stake in one of the international oil consortiums there. U.S. companies are not permitted to participate in any project in which an Iranian company has a stake, hence, threatening any U.S. participation in developing the Caspian Sea resources. This could actually mean that U.S. companies could become potential liabilities in regard to Caspian Sea projects, even where there is no current Iranian participation, because any future Iranian participation would force the U.S. partner to leave the project. This would put current U.S. sanctions policy in conflict with the current U.S. policy of encouraging U.S. participation in the development of Caspian Sea oil and gas resources. At a recent oil industry conference, Deputy Assistant Secretary of State Ramsey, who is in charge of sanctions, pointed out that "the cost of sanctions can be very high" for U.S. business.

This raises the question, do these costs bring commensurate benefits for the United States? Let us look at them in summary.

- Our Iranian-Libyan oil sanctions policy will remain unilateral, notwithstanding the recent headline-grabbing German court decision.
- The effectiveness of our secondary sanctions policy is quite limited, both because most foreign countries oppose them and may take retaliatory action, and because foreign firms with no stake in the U.S. are generally beyond their reach.
- Finally, Iran has operated its oil industry without foreign participation since the revolution of 1979, and its current export level is at least being maintained, and probably will be increased.

Thus, in regard to the question of who gets hurt more by our sanctions policy, the targeted country or the U.S. companies excluded from doing business with it, the answer may not be one that is supportive of our current policy. Thank you.

Questions and Answers

MR. HENRY PRECHT (Former Country Director for Iran, State Department): To the members of the panel, I would like to pose two questions. The first has to do with the financial means available to Iran for pursuing weapons of mass destruction through conventional build-up, and for achieving contentment at home. Does Iran have the resources required for it to undertake all of those tasks in a meaningful way?

Secondly, with the example of the destruction inflicted upon Iraq in response to its invasion of Kuwait, would Iran undertake policies that would likely bring that kind of destruction to its own countryside, at the same time as it is making major investments?

DR. ANTHONY CORDESMAN (Middle East Studies Program, Center for Strategic & International Studies): Let me try to deal with just the technical aspects of this question. First, proliferation is relatively cheap. It is relatively cheap because biological weapons are cheap, because you are moving into an era where many of the components of long-range cruise missiles are becoming commercially available, and it is cheap because you have already a major infrastructure for chemical weapons and pharmaceuticals.

The issue of nuclear proliferation is much more complex than it sometimes appears. In general it has never been the money that has been the problem, or the basic technology; but rather, the fact that developing states simply cannot create efficient chains or structures. Iraq is a good case in point. The first United Nations reports were very, very dramatic. What was fascinating was that, as time went on, Iraq put billions of dollars into large-scale enrichment facilities, and neither the Yemus program nor the Centrifuge program, as constituted, would ever have worked. If you can buy nuclear fissile material, it is cheap.

In regard to conventional military forces, it is incredibly expensive to launch a broad-based military build-up. But what Iran is doing in the Gulf is relatively cheap. Certainly sanctions will not influence a steadily more sophisticated build-up in that area.

In terms of your last point, it is very difficult for me to see how there could be a deliberate repetition of the Gulf War. Iran does not have a common-land border with the Southern Gulf, that it is contained by its neighbor, Iraq, and that its power projection capabilities are not only limited, but do not seem to be tied to any intent to use them.

Historically, the problem would be whether both sides over-escalate, and if what starts out as a moderate military action goes too far. However, during 1987 and 1988 we demonstrated that we can peacefully coexist while fighting. Without any attempt to be facetious about it and all rhetoric aside, I think we can live with the kinds of clashes that are likely.

DR. GARY SICK (Gulf 2000 Project, Columbia University): In Iran, as elsewhere, the regime is primarily concerned about its own survival. That is what it thinks about first, and that is what it is really interested in. In the earliest days of the revolution, that meant being as revolutionary, as Islamic, as outrageous as possible, because that was where the regime saw its legitimization coming from; that is how it justified itself.

As time has gone on, much of that fire has gone out of the revolution, and the leaders face very prosaic questions about where they should put their resources. What do they use their resources for? To preserve themselves and to strengthen the regime? Increasingly, the regime has been making these decisions in terms of domestic development, keeping the basic constituency happy.

We largely ignore the fact that the Iranian government has provided almost all of the villages in Iran with access to electricity, that there are now gas lines serving the villages, and that there are roads in places that were never there before. A tremendous amount of money has gone into these initiatives.

When it comes to the nuclear issue, Iran's officials must ask themselves if achieving nuclear armament is worth it, in terms of diverting money away from some other type of investment. This remains an open question.

I agree with Dr. Cordesman that we tend to see things in stark black-and-white terms, that we tend to be confident that this is the only way it can go, that this is the only answer. Yet, in fact, I genuinely believe that there is a real division within the Iranian leadership about which direction they should take on the subject of nuclear build-up. It does not seem to be the case at all that Iran's leaders are all agreed and in favor of nuclear weapons. The fact that we do have some problems with evidence is, in fact, evidence that Iran's policy is still in flux.

I had a conversation with a Pakistani fellow who was very closely involved with his country's nuclear development program. I asked him, "What is your take on the Iranian effort?" He responded, ¡Oh, they are buying some stuff. . . . But I can tell you, they have not really put much of a team together, because if they did, we would be running into them. We are mining the same territory, we are trying to talk to the same people, and we would be in fact stepping on each other's toes." He stated that, "It is not happening. The Iranians are out there, but," he said, "it is a very low-level thing."

Now, from my point of view, this does not mean that the Iranians are being good guys. They are making their decisions in terms of their own domestic needs and long-term defense needs. But, if it is true, it does provide an opportunity for encouraging those folks on the side who would rather not be putting their money into nuclear programs, rather than pushing the people who do believe in nuclear build-up, pushing them hard and forcing them into it.

Again, the tendency has been to view the issues in stark black and white is the issue. It is not so much a matter of just demonization. If it is blind demonization, it is wrong. If it is sanctification, in Dr. Cordesman's words, that is equally wrong. That is not the way it should be.

There is gray area. This is a complicated government, made up of many different coalitions. What bothers me about U.S. policy is that we are making no effort to work with that complexity. We are trying to simplify it and make it all bad or all good. And that simply is not going to work.

Opportunities for trade-off are presenting themselves, but we are not taking advantage of them. If the goal is to keep Iran from developing nuclear weaponry, now is the time to act, before they have made much progress. Act now, rather than play the game that we played in North Korea, where we waited until we thought they had a bomb before we panicked at the last minute and paid them off to stop. Now is a much better time to act.

DR. JOHN LICHTBLAU (Petroleum Research Foundation): I will comment briefly. I think it might help to tie Iran more to private foreign investments — Western investments, I am talking about. As we have pointed out, Iran has a basic need for a substantial increase in investments in its oil and gas.

This has a psychological aspect to it. If Westerners come in, if there is Western technology and equipment, and if there is an interchange of technical and other discussion, I believe this will open up the country. Presently we have succeeded in closing Iran and we are trying to shut it out even more. This increases the hostility, the fear, and the assumption that out there is the enemy.

So if a move were made in the other direction, I believe that it not only would be important as far as the oil sector itself is concerned, but it would create possibly a different attitude in Iran. We have seen this happen in the past, when there were foreign investments, some from the West. I think that opening up relations with Iran holds the possibility of significant side effects in terms of training, contacts and so on. By removing the possibility of these contacts, in my opinion, we are moving in the wrong direction.

MR. RICHARD PARKER (Middle East Institute): Today, I am speaking in my capacity as a substitute "Joe Six-Pack". My experience with "Joe Six-Pack" is that he does not know the difference between Iraq and Iran, and he thinks the Iranians are Arabs. (I never know who is most insulted by this, the Persians or the Arabs!) But he does not pay much attention to the questions which we are discussing.

I quite agree, and am very impressed with Steve Rosen's very eloquent description of Iranian terrorist activities. But clearly our policy is, in a larger sense, a function of our relationship with Israel. However, my question is, what has changed Israelís attitude? After all, the Israelis were supplying Iran with military equipment as late as 1984 and 1985, and they were instrumental in our involvement in Irangate. What has changed their attitude toward Iran, and, would that change our policy towards Iran?

MR. STEVEN ROSEN (American Israeli Political Action Committee): I think that Israelis are deeply divided about many questions, as everybody knows. Yet striking similarities emerge when one engages at length in serious, private discussion with security officials whose private beliefs are associated with the Labor and Likud Parties, or with factions to the left of Labor or with parties to the right of Likud. Just as there is a homogeneity of opinion in this room on one side of the question, the Israeli officials - all of them - are convinced that the Iranians are employing a wide variety of means as they engage in a systematic effort aimed at Israel. There is consensus that the Iranians are serious about destroying moderate leadership in the Arab side, Israel's peace partners; that the Iranians did play a key role in bringing Shimon Perez down; that they are trying to eliminate the Palestinian leadership; and that, in the long run and if nothing changes, there will be an extreme military confrontation between Iran and Israel, brought about by Iran.

When he was alive, Itzak Rabin said that the reason he was prepared to take what were some fairly sweeping and very difficult risks for peace, not only with the Palestinians but particularly with the Syrians, was that, as he put it, "We have seven years, if we are lucky, and then we are going to be in the most difficult struggle in our history. A true existential war, from Israelís point of view. We have to do what we can to pare away the immediate problems with the closer-in neighbors, particularly Syria, and to bring an end to the inner war, so we can concentrate all our resources on this." Rabin said this in private - I am not speaking of propaganda speeches - and these views seemed to be at the root of his willingness to go remarkably far, actually, in the scope of concessions he was prepared to make to Syria.

In response to the last part of your question, first let me point out that I work for a pro-Israel organization and believe deeply in it. However, I do not think that the issue of Israel is by any means the only reason we should be concerned about Iran.

Let us examine the case of Iraq. The community of scholars did not really expect Iraq to strike. When the attack occurred, it was directed toward Kuwait in the first instance, not Israel, and when Iraqi missiles rained on Tel Aviv, at the same time missiles were aimed at Riyadh. In the case of Iran, we see already that it is targeting Saudi Arabia, the United Arab Emirates and Bahrain. If Israel ceased to be an issue in this regard, I do not believe that the United States' concern over the growth of Iranian power would diminish. Israel is only one part of the issue.

DR. GARY SICK (Gulf 2000 Project, Columbia University): I do not pretend to be an expert on Israel, but I do think there is a further answer to your question, Mr. Parker. Israel was indeed supporting Iran for many years, selling them arms and cooperating with them. The relationship was extremely close, as we know - including joint efforts toward research and development of missile systems - and actually continued after the revolution, certainly on through Irangate, in the mid-1980's. It came to an end, in my view, after the second Gulf War when Iraq was brought under control and was less of a threat to Israel. At the same time, Labor was pushing very hard for an opening to the Arab states, instead of seeing the Arabs as totally hostile. So suddenly there was a different attitude, and Israel's "Doctrine of the Periphery", or the idea of balancing off Iraq with Iran, was no longer such an attractive proposition.

After Netanyahu came in, a whole different set of issues arose, tactically. First, I think Netanyahu is not so willing to count on a friendly group of Arabs around him, not in the same way that Shimon Peres was. Since July of last year, Netanyahu has not publicly said a bad word about Iran. In July, indirect contacts via Germany helped to arrange a swap of bodies for prisoners in Lebanon. Since then Netanyahu has pursued a somewhat different approach. I do not call this an opening to Iran because I do not think Israel's basic strategic views have changed. However, the tactics are different. I think Israel is quite capable of changing its tactics, depending on its own perception of what it needs. I think we are less able to do that.

MS. LAURIE LANDE (Dow Jones): During the Bush Administration we saw a build-up of trade with Iran, and in fact a promotion of ties with Iran. What was the major factor that changed this course so radically? Obviously the end of the Cold War had something to do with it. But I would be curious to hear Mr. Precht's perspective, as well as those of the others, as to what the main factors were that caused such a radical change in our policy, from the Bush Administration to the Clinton Administration.

MR. STEVEN ROSEN (American Israeli Political Action Committee): Ms. Lande, I will respond to your question in a moment. First, I would like to say a word about Netanyahu and Iran. I think there has been a considerable amount of confusion on this subject.

I do not represent the government of Israel, nor does the Near East Report. Since Israel does not have representatives here, let me tell you that if they were in the room, you would have heard a rather strong response. It is definitely not the case that an opening has been extended to Iran by the Netanyahu government. If anything, quite the reverse. The government is increasingly alarmed about Iran. The Prime Minister and his advisors made a tactical decision to lower the rhetorical level, based on the theory that Israel has major immediate problems with its neighbors and that only the United States is able to take on Iran. Israel is too far away, and, it does not want to be the primary focus of Islamic fervor.

As a result of this decision, there was silence on the issue. Behind the scenes, the policy, in fact, was hardening, and, I believe that recently the Israeli government has concluded that this is not possible. Recent statements made by the Prime Minister and the Foreign Minister have been replete with comments of this kind. For instance, 10 days ago the Prime Minister said, "We can take care of the problem of the Syrians and Palestinians diplomatically. But in the long run, the threat to Israel's existence . . ." he said, ". . . is Iran. And this threat is growing and getting much worse."

As far as the change from the Bush to the Clinton Administrations is concerned, the previous administration allowed a situation to develop in which American companies became the number-one trading partners of Iran. They primarily were engaged in buying Iranian oil and reselling it to third parties, rather than importing it into the United States.

When President Clinton urged the Europeans, particularly the Germans, to tighten up their policies toward Iran, Helmut Kohl commented to the President, in an exchange that apparently had a shock effect on him, "Why are you telling me this? Your companies are number one, have become number one. They have now outstripped us, surpassed our companies." The President ordered an internal review to see whether this was true, and of course it turned out to be true. The increase in trade that had taken place under Mr. Scowcroft in the Bush years created a consensus that something had to be done. Subsequently, President Clinton not only blocked the Conoco deal in one Executive Order, but all trade in a second. So I think that that was probably the single most important source of the policy shift.

MS. MARIE YARED (Amoco): This question is for Dr. Cordesman. You mentioned that Syria is a significant evil in the area. How do you envision a post-Assad Syria, a post-Assad Middle East . . .given that he does not have a clear succession at this point.

DR. ANTHONY CORDESMAN (Middle East Studies Program, Center for Strategic & International Studies): I do not think I used the word "evil," I think I used the word "influence" in reference to the major role played by Syria. Nations in this region are acting according to their own perceived strategic interests, and the fact that we regard them as hostile is not necessarily a measure of moral values.

Right now in Syria, a set of economic reforms which appeared to be significant and had the potential of moving the society forward have gotten hung up, and are really not progressing. I would have said that the more Syria modernized and privatized, the more stable its structure would be, in a post-Assad environment. I am not reassured that Assad put his son through a military academy. This reminds me of Saddam Hussein acquiring a military uniform after getting through law school. It indicates that we may not get rid of the Assad family when Hafez dies. Frankly, these inherited regimes are not particularly stable, and they often make things worse.

Having said that, what I do not see is Syria becoming a state which is divided either into some revival of Sunni Islamic extremism, or an open conflict between the Alevis and the secular Sunnis. I think it is likely to just slowly evolve out of Assadís death, without radically changing any of its attitudes or behavior patterns.

I also have to say, frankly, that unless the Syrians do much more in terms of their economy, the birth rate in the country is so high that, over the next five to ten years, the society will degenerate sharply, regardless of who the leader is.

MR. KENNETH TIMMERMAN (Iran Brief): Dr. Cordesman, in regard to your comment about assassination of Iranian dissidents overseas, I found it frankly bizarre that the suggestion was made that they are the violent opponents of the regime. In fact, there are scores and scores of Iranian exiles who have been killed who were journalists, human rights activists, and what have you. These assassinations have continued up to the present time. Thousands inside Iran have been killed by the regime, as well. Recently a whole series of writers and journalists were attacked, during a renewed crackdown.

The Mykonos case in Germany, which has received little comment this morning, has begun to change the way the Europeans are looking at Iran's regime. As a result of the regime's human rights violations and its aggressive campaign of terrorism overseas, I believe that we might see some inflection in European policy.

DR. ANTHONY CORDESMAN (Middle East Studies Program, Center for Strategic & International Studies): Could I comment, please? I strongly dislike being flatly misquoted. I was very clear to distinguish that there were two sets of terrorist activities, and that the terrorist strikes against the peaceful opposition were just that. I repeated this three or four times. I referred specifically to the State Department Report on Human Rights as an example of a critical yet objective report of many types of activities which Iran should discontinue. If this is somehow to get around to glorifying Rajavi and company, Ken, the hell with them.

MR. TIMMERMAN: I agree with you on that point.

MR. JEAN-MARA OPPENHEIM: Thank you. I do not have the statistics, but it is common knowledge that in Iran there are very large numbers of graduates of American universities, probably the largest number of American university graduates in the world. These graduates hold positions in the professions, the bureaucracy, and in technology. In what ways can the U.S. mine these potential allies as they exist within the Iranian regime, now or after the elections?

DR. GARY SICK: First, Mr. Oppenheim, graduates of American universities are not necessarily pro-American. In fact, some of the most radical opponents of the United States in various countries around the world have graduated from universities in America. We have radicalized whole generations of people in other countries. So I think that it is false to assume that these graduates would be allies.

Secondly, however, there are Iranians who would like to see improved relations with the United States. Let me just describe a conversation that I had with a very senior Iranian official not too long ago, who made the following observations: "You know, we have been 18 years now with zero contact, and there is a new generation coming along." He continued, by saying, "People like me —I went to school in the United States. I have a strong personal feeling about the

United States, and think that it is even worth taking some risks to try to make things better between us."

But, as he went on to say, "There is another generation just behind me that does not share any of that, that has no such memories, and says why should we even bother with any kind of relations with the United States? Why is it worth taking any risks to do this?" And, as he said, "Time is passing".

It is possible to begin to develop and maintain personal contacts, and many persons in this room are, in fact, doing this on a fairly regular basis. However, things do not change overnight.

Let me just finish up by addressing a point made by Mr. Rosen at the beginning. He suggested that, in effect, the experts are always wrong; that if you have got a bunch of intellectuals and they all agree that this is the way it is going to go, it has got to go some other way; that basically, Joe Six-Pack knows better. Well, that is garbage. Consider the following example:

The Iran-Libya Sanctions Act was actively debated in the United States Congress, specifically in regard to the question of whether it was a good idea to impose secondary sanctions, with the memory of the fact that we had opposed secondary sanctions for so long with regard to Israel.

As this debate continued, TWA flight #800 crashed off the coast of Long Island. All debate ceased and the bill was passed unanimously. Some might argue that the bill's passage resulted from the crash of TWA flight #800, because at the time, Iranian terrorism was suddenly suspected as a factor. The proposed bill was bad, and was passed for the wrong reason. This provides an example of this whole demonization process.

The Oklahoma City bombing provides a second example of this process. After the bombing, there were so-called experts —Daniel Pipes was one — who rushed to say it was an Iranian attack against the United States, . . . that they were coming after us. Comments such as these were quoted in the media. Well, they all turned out to be wrong about those things.

This whole business of reviving the language of the Cold War and turning it into a debate is really not helpful. Iran does some things that we dislike and oppose, with reason. But the way we are going about dealing with it, painting it all with one color, is not going to end the process, and in fact, could make it worse.

PANEL II:
EUROPEAN, RUSSIAN, AND CANADIAN PERSPECTIVES

Opening Remarks

Julia Nanay (Panel Chair)
Director, Petroleum Finance Company

When I was asked a couple of weeks ago to chair this panel, I was extremely pleased, given the timeliness of the subject being discussed.

The speakers on this panel are all highly experienced diplomats when it comes to issues dealing with the Middle East. Given the current debate going on in the United States about sanctions policy in Iran, I am sure that the different approaches of the countries represented on this panel will help to further frame this debate.

Each of today's panelists has a critical role to play with regard to Iran. These roles are complementary in some ways, particularly because all of the respective governments maintain some level of political and economic ties with Iran, even though they may have dissimilar views. Before moving on to our speakers, I would like to set the stage by providing background information on some of the issues which drive the various approaches to our subject, as addressed by our panelists.

First, I would like to say a few words about Russia. It is probably fair to say that Russia is developing the closest political ties, based upon certain shared economic interests in the region as well as upon the mutual goal of building a regional political military grouping to offset the United States.

Perceiving itself to be hemmed in on the west by the U.S. and NATO, Russia is moving east to form a new superpower alliance with both Iran and China. As the U.S. feels pressure to further isolate Iran, the Russian-Iranian alliance draws closer. For example, Iran has purchased for its Navy three Russian submarines, which are now stationed in the Straits of Hormuz, an important shipping lane for oil. Iran has also purchased missiles from Russia, and Russia is helping Iran build a nuclear power plant.

As someone who is working on oil and gas issues, I consider to be of particular significance for Western oil companies the fact that Iran and Russia are cooperating on delineating the Caspian Sea, arguing for joint development, by the five bordering countries, of resources that fall outside of a 45-mile off-shore limit. This could jeopardize the major oil development currently underway in Azerbaijan, the AIOC project.

Another interesting development on the energy front is that just this past week Russia's gas company, Gazprom, signed agreements with Iran to help in gas field development. Given that Russia and Iran together control close to 50 percent of the world's gas reserves, their cooperation could have certain complications for future access to Iran's vast reserves by Western companies. For example, if Western companies are prevented from concluding deals in Iran because of the U.S. sanction pressure, Gazprom may try to fill the void. In addition, Russian oil companies have agreed to spread their drilling activities to Iran's portion of the Caspian Sea.

One thing that strikes me is that Iran now seems to be in a position, with Russia's help, to arbitrate oil flows from the Persian Gulf to the Straits of Hormoz. In addition, the two countries together will determine the flow of oil from the Caspian. This has important implications for the world's current and future supplies of oil.

Second, if we turn to the European Union, which is also represented here, we might note that it is the EU that is supposed to play a growing role in the United States' plan to isolate Iran. So far, European countries still have extensive trade relations with Iran, and European companies continue to negotiate for oil and gas deals in both Iran and Iraq. The 15 countries of the EU exported about $5 billion in goods to Iran in 1996, and they imported $6 billion worth of goods. This resulted in about a billion-dollar trade surplus for Iran. The EU collectively buys about 10 percent of its imported oil needs from Iran. This in turn accounts for over a third of Iran's oil exports.

The Mykonos verdict in Germany on April 10, 1997 implicated Iran in the killings of three Kurdish dissidents and their interpreter in a Berlin restaurant in 1992. While this verdict has thrown European-Iranian relations into a brief tailspin, the general view is that the storm will blow over, and a gradual easing of tensions will occur.

The United States sees the German ruling as an opportunity

to rally the EU behind a much tougher U.S. position — U.S. Secretary of State Madeline Albright's envoy, Peter Tarnoff, has been touring European capitols this week to put pressure on those governments to tow the U.S. line. The EU is scheduled to hold a meeting on this subject in just a few days, on April 29, in Luxembourg.

Next on our panel, Canada is also represented. While Canada conducts some trade with Iran, its importance here may not be related particularly to the trade issue. In my opinion — and I am sure there are those who might question this link— it is not an arbitrary coincidence that the U.S.' temporary easing of enforcement of the Helms-Burton Law, which targets Cuba where Canadian and European companies are active, was announced at virtually the same time that Germany came out with the Mykonos ruling. I think one event may have been a quid pro quo for the other. The United States made some concessions, at least temporarily, in regard to Cuba, while Europe acted similarly in regard to Iran.

This can be seen as a double-edged victory, and certainly with regard to Helms-Burton, a victory for Canada. In point of fact, however, Europe may be prevented from returning to its critical dialogue policy with Iran if the United States decides to launch a military action. The linchpin seems to be two Sunni- Saudi detainees in Canada, who were arrested in March by Canadian authorities when they tried to enter that country. They may provide the U.S. with the evidence it needs to tie Iran to the bombing last June in Saudi Arabia where 19 servicemen from the U.S. were killed. If the United States decides that the evidence is adequate to point a finger at Iran in that incident, it could launch an attack, possibly targeting Iran's oil facilities. This could seriously upset oil markets, driving prices up, and it would obviously also derail all trade and investment activity with Iran for the immediate future.

Finally, we have the Bosnian angle represented here. As you may all recall, there has been considerable political uproar in the U.S. over Iranian arms shipments to Bosnia, condoned by the Clinton Administration in the early 1990s. This facilitated Bosnia's ability to defend itself against Serbia.

Our distinguished panel includes:

- Mr. Michael. Konarovsky, Counselor at the Russian

Embassy in Washington for Middle East, Southwest, and Central Asian Affairs
- Mr. Stefan Van-Wersch, First Secretary of the Dutch Embassy in Washington, where he represents the European Union Presidency, which is currently held by the Netherlands
- Mr. Stuart Hughes, Counselor (Political) at the Canadian Embassy in Washington, where he handles relations with the US, vis-à-vis the Middle East
- Mr. Nadzib Sacirbey, the Ambassador-at-Large for Bosnia-Herzegovina

Each of these panelists will present his views on the issues I have discussed above, and others. Perhaps it would be best if we wait until all panelists have finished before the floor is opened to questions. First I would like to call on Mr. Konarovsky.

Russian-Iranian Relations

Michael Konarovsky
Counsellor, Russian Embassy

Thanks for inviting me to speak. I understand the interest which has been shown here and in the United States in general, in reference to Russian-Iranian relations; a source of disagreement between our two governments.

In regard to this, I would like to stress two main points. Point number one has to do with the fact that Iran is an immediate neighbor of the Russian Federation. Russian policy is aimed at having smooth, predictable, balanced and comprehensive relations with all its neighbors; not only CIS, but also such nations as China, Turkey, Iran, Mongolia and others. This is a very important point for our present and future policy, of course.

We have had a long-term relationship with Iran, and it is worth remembering that, despite many ups and downs, the former Soviet Union had smooth relations with the Shah of Iran. We have had comprehensive economic dealings with Iran, which have expanded, especially since the mid-1960s, after the Shah declined to deploy nuclear arms on Iranian soil. Both countries understood that it was to their mutual benefit to maintain normal relations, despite political differences between the former Soviet Union and the Shah's regime.

The same approach was followed by the former Soviet Union after the fall of the Shah and the Islamic Revolution. But immediately after the new regime was installed in Tehran, relations between Iran and Russia declined because of Iran's approach to the Soviet Union, which was seen in Tehran as a "devil" second to the United States. But despite that fact, the Soviet Union tried to continue and maintain relations with Iranians, and this brought success when, in the late eighties, Ayatollah Khomeini sent a message to President Gorbochev, suggesting the re-establishment of neighborly relations. The Soviet Union accepted immediately. I would like to mention that the bulk of the understandings and agreements which Russia has now with Iran have stemmed from that period of time.

Russia is very much interested in maintaining economic and

trade relations with Iran, which is a very important trade partner for the Russian Federation. These economic ties are very deep-rooted. Russia has common interests with Iran on a number of international and regional issues. Primary, in my view, is our common interest in the resources of the Caspian Sea. Both Russia and Iran are littoral nations, and are eligible to discuss, with all other neighbors, how these tremendous resources should be used in the future, to the benefit of all. We share the view that it is necessary for the littoral nations to discuss these matters among themselves, and to come to mutual understanding and agreement. For example, Iran has cooperated in resolving the Tajik crisis and in achieving a peaceful resolution of the situation in Afghanistan. As you know, the political headquarters of forces opposing the Tajik government are located in Tehran. Iranians are positively active in trying to bring the parties to mutual understanding, and Tehran is helpful in the peace process in Tajikistan. Russia shares with Iran a necessity for Afghanistan to stop fighting and to have a broad-based government that will represent the interests of all the ethnic and religious communities of that country.

My second major point is that the Russian government does not share the view of those governments who consider Iran to be a rogue state and who advocate for the isolation of Iran. We consider such an approach absolutely unproductive, both for Iran and for those who are seeking to isolate it in the international arena. That is why Russia, in my view, will not support any kind of sanctions against Iran in the future, and will continue its policy of maintaining comprehensive relations with Tehran.

Of great importance is the fact that we speak with Iranians about the necessity of observing international norms of behavior. We believe that normal relations between our two countries might be of much help in this respect.

Just recently the President of the Iranian Parliament, Mr. Nateq Nuri, visited Russia at the invitation of the Duma, and was received by President Yeltsin. He had received a preliminary invitation from the Duma last year when a delegation from the State Duma visited in Tehran. His arrival in Moscow at the time of the Mykonos trial must not be considered as some sort of specific anti-western gesture on behalf of the Russians.

During his visit, a number of international issues, including Tajikistan and Afghanistan, were discussed. We spoke about the experience to further bilateral relations as well. What is very important is that a protocol of understanding on export control was signed, which in my view gives Russia, if neccessary, more leverage to influence the Iranians in order to achieve strict observation of the obligations assumed by that country according to the NPT. Thank you.

The European Union and Iran

Stefan Van-Wersch
First Secretary, Embassy of the Netherlands
(Current European Union President)

Ladies and gentlemen, let me first stress that it is indeed an honor and a pleasure to speak at this conference, organized by highly reputable organizations such as Rutgers University and the Middle East Institute.

There is in Washington sometimes a certain tendency to overlook the stance of the European Union on certain matters. I commend the organizers of this conference for not making this mistake. It is also a challenge to explain EU policy towards Iran and the United States, and indeed it bears a certain resemblance to a mission under Chapter VII of the United Nations Charter, operating in a not-really-permissive environment. One tends to encounter strong negative feelings in the United States on the EU policy towards Iran. Some observations from the EU perspective, and as I hope, an open and frank discussion afterwards, are therefore appropriate. In fact, a discussion of both the U.S. and EU policies, and their interaction, seem most timely in view of recent events.

This challenge is, however, not the real problem today. It is rather that the EU policy is in a temporary limbo due to recent developments; namely, the verdict, as you know, of the German Court in the Mykonos case. Subsequent to the verdict, the European Union has suspended its critical dialogue with Iran, and recalled its ambassadors for consultation. In its declaration, the Union underlined that it has always wanted a constructive relationship with Iran, but that progress in this field has been impossible while Iran flouts international norms and engages in acts of terrorism.

By the way, in view of some comments in the U.S. media in the style of "we told you so," I would like to remark that the Mykonos verdict did not surprise the European Union. Iran's involvement in acts like the Mykonos assassinations, which, between brackets, predated the critical dialogue, was rather one of the reasons to engage in the dialogue. So the reply "we told you so" and remarks of that type can provoke the response of, "Thanks, anyhow, but we already knew."

The recalled ambassadors have not yet returned to Iran, in view of further consultations within the EU framework. The pivotal discussion on the political level is scheduled for the next Tuesday [April 29, 1997], when the General Affairs Council, the EU meeting of Ministers of Foreign Affairs, will meet in Brussels. Until then, there is no clarity on the European policy, which does not make it particularly easy for me to address you today.

Still, some observations can be made. This critical dialogue, Europe's policy of constructive engagement with Iran, has been suspended, and probably will remain suspended for still some time. But it has not been canceled. Full cancellation is, in my assessment, quite unlikely. It remains, therefore, worthwhile to discuss the background of this dialogue, which has proven to be an unfortunate wrinkle in the EU-US relationship.

Let me first emphasize that the U.S. and EU assessments of Iranian policy overlap to a very high degree. Both strive to improve Iran's behavior, ultimately aiming at a full Iranian observance of international law. In the critical dialogue, the EU has consistently tabled the many issues that form the core of U.S. concerns, namely, Iranian involvement in terrorism and its amassing an arsenal of both conventional and non-conventional arms among which are weapons of mass destruction. Other issues have included the Iranian opposition to the peace process, Iran's poor human rights record, and the fatwa against Salman Rushdie.

Be assured that this dialogue, which is sometimes in the U.S. portrayed as a kind of open-ended, non-committal chat of ministers, has indeed been very critical. I am not in a position, as you can understand, to distribute the read-outs of these meetings. But let there be no misunderstanding on the tone. I underline further that the U.S. has never excluded the possibility of having a dialogue with Iran, a so-called authorized dialogue. The EU considers its policy, therefore, not as contrary to the U.S. policy, but rather as complementary. The policy differences are not about the assessment of the problem, nor the ultimate goal, but about the means to reach the goal. In the EU's judgment, an isolation of Iran by economic measures or sanctions, as pursued by the U.S. in its containment policy, would not attain the desirable goals we all share.

Let me add that my next remark is a personal one. I cannot predict what will be the exact outcome of the General Affairs Council next Monday. But I would be amazed if the EU policy on this point will fundamentally change, since the arguments for it are still as valid as before.

Iran's importance in the region, its size, its increasing number of inhabitants, resources, geographic position, and its role as a regional power make the isolation of Iran both impossible and undesirable. It would be a sheer illusion to think that sanctions, even if they would be broader than just the unilateral U.S. boycott, would be effective and bring the Iranian government to its knees.

Let's be frank. There is not much evidence in recent history that sanctions of this kind lead to the desired aims. From a purely functional point of view, they might be successfully implemented, as for instance, cut off oil exports. Politically, however, the results tend to be far less conspicuous. And then I leave aside the sometimes alarming humanitarian consequences. In the EU's judgment, an isolation policy might rather have the reverse effect, and stiffen Iran in its defiance.

Let me just mention one element. As you know, anti-Western feelings constitute part of the hard core of the fundamentalist creed. Isolating Iran, rather than engaging it in a dialogue, however difficult and discouraging, would only fulfill the fundamentalist prophesies; and by virtue of that, bolster the hard-line elements in the government.

In general, the EU attaches a very high importance to a dialogue with Islamic countries, which are the EU's direct neighbors. The EU has always believed, without harboring any illusions on this point, that a dialogue in which all issues are brought to the table, stands a better chance of having a moderating influence on Iran, in the long run — and I repeat, in the long run, than a containment policy. The EU has further held the belief that this critical dialogue can go together with economic and commercial ties. Economic ties might even reinforce the dialogue by increasing Iran's interaction with the international market, and by encouraging economic reform toward a free market economy.

Let me add that more examples can be given of countries whose human rights records are criticized by the EU, even though economic and commercial ties are maintained. For that matter the United States maintains economic and commercial ties with certain countries, while, simultaneously, it criticizes their human rights records.

For the record, and for those who believe that the EU policy is cynically and exclusively geared towards commercial goals, I would note that for most EU states Iran is not a really important trade partner, and that EU exports to Iran have shown a downward movement in recent years.

I add that, for instance, for the Netherlands, a pre-eminently exporting country, Iran is really not an important trade partner. And still we have always backed the critical dialogue. So we do not have direct commercial reasons for a policy of this kind. It would be too simple just to equate two things, commercial interest and critical dialogue.

Further, it is my personal assessment that in general, there seems to be more grass-roots support in the U.S. for policies of isolation and economic sanctions than in Europe, where the belief prevails that suspension of free trade will not change the behavior of rogue states. Probably this has also to do with a different cultural mentality towards questions like how to deal with difficult states.

At this point I do not want to omit mentioning that there is full consensus in Europe on one other point; namely, that U.S. legislation designed order to force third states to comply with U.S. policy toward Iran [the so-called secondary sanctions], is considered fully unacceptable in principle. Legislation of this kind is not conducive to a common EU-U.S. policy stance on Iran. We do not like it when our policy is being made in Washington. And I would like to see the outrage if it were the other way around.

All this does not mean that the critical dialogue until now has been particularly successful. Results are limited, though not absent — we did not expect fast results, by the way. But they are not absent. I refer to Iran's signing the Chemical Weapons Treaty for which the EU wants to take some credit, the prolongation of the Non-Proliferation Treaty, Iranís cooperation with the IAEA (International Atomic Energy Agency), and some humanitarian cases.

The importance of having a channel to put pressure on Iran with regard to human rights issues should not be underestimated.

Overall, the dialogue, however, has undeniably been a discouraging experience for those engaged in it. Under the current circumstances, it is not a viable way of engaging Iran. The current crisis has proved that the critical dialogue itself needs a critical assessment. The European Council meeting in Luxembourg (April 1996) has already underlined that the critical dialogue has to become more results-oriented. Member states' parliaments and the public, which are particularly sensitive to the lack of progress in the Rushdie case, have expressed irritation with regard to the lack of concrete results.

As I explained above, I do not believe that the EU will give up the concept of a critical dialogue, which, from the methodological point of view, is still considered the most effective policy. But within the concept there is space for adjustment. More sticks might be added to the carrots.

Further, we seem to have reached a crucial juncture, opening possibilities for a closer coordination and convergence between U.S. and EU policies. The results of the critical dialogue may be poor, but we should not forget that the same goes for the U.S. policy. Both parties have reached a stage where rethinking is appropriate, and a renewed bid for closer cooperation logical.

Iran should indeed not be allowed to live under the impression that it can drive a wedge between the U.S. and EU. In fact, closer coordination is already underway. Let me add, at the end of this short discourse, one observation that is often overlooked in the United States. The media and some think tanks in the U.S. regularly urge the EU to follow the U.S. policy. In my assessment, more convergence is possible, but a mere signing on to the U.S. sanction policy is at present not in the books.

The EU is a union of 15 member states which do not have the exact same ideas on dealing with Iran, nor the same interests. The critical dialogue has proven to be the common denominator on which the 15 were able to have a common policy. The alternative to this policy is not something similar to the U.S. policy, but rather, the end of a common policy. And, instead of it, there would be 15 more or less competing policies, of which some might even be more disliked by the United States than the critical dialogue. This, of course, would definitely not serve our common goals, but only play into the Iranian hands. I thank you.

Canada's Policy Toward Iran

Stuart Hughes
Counsellor (Political), The Canadian Embassy

I would like to commend the organizers of today's meeting for bringing together officials and other experts to share ideas on how the West and the Russian Federation deal with Iran. The topic is enormous. As this morning's panels so amply illustrated, it is as complex as any foreign policy community faces. Moreover, the timing of today's gathering could not be better, given recent events in Europe and in the region.

My aim is to provide you with some background on Canada's policy towards Iran and to outline, in broad terms, our current approach. I would emphasize that these are my own views, and not necessarily the definitive word from Ottawa, not least because the West's relations with Iran are evolving as we speak.

To put matters in context, if there is one word that characterizes Canada's relations with Iran, that word would be regret. Why? Let me offer a few reasons.

First, Iran is home to one of the world's oldest civilizations, and of course, it is a great center of Islam. It is a country of some 60 million people, and remains one of the most important in Asia. Second, Iran has serious economic potential and enormous hydrocarbon resources. Third, with its people and resources, Iran could be a major force for the good, for stability in the region, and an international leader in social and economic development in a world that badly needs it.

But regrettably, as seen from Canada, Iran has a very long way to go. We believe that Iran must resume its place in the family of nations, but we also believe, and we believe adamantly, that this is possible only if the government of Iran shows, in word and deed, that it respects the norms of interstate behavior.

There is nothing particularly new in that position. Canada has not had normalized relations with Iran since the revolution. We have restricted the sale of military or otherwise sensitive dual-use products since the Iran-Iraq War. Our Embassy was closed for a number of years after the hostage-taking, when, as you recall, Canada played a singular role in ensuring that those who took refuge in our Ambassador's residence reached safety. That Embassy only reopened in 1988, and today we do have an Ambassador in Tehran.

We also have maintained strict controls on political relations. In recent years there have been little, very little, ministerial interaction, and few meetings among officials at the Director-General level. Although our trade is significant, we do not have a joint economic commission. There are no official parliamentary exchanges, although Canadian Parliamentarians have visited Iran privately. And our scientific contacts are minimal.

Those issues of concern to us, which others have expressed eloquently this morning, are Iran's human rights record with regard to religious minorities, like the Bahais, intellectuals, and others. It includes Iran's support of terrorism, and the assassination of dissidents abroad, Iran's unwillingness to halt its pursuit of weapons of mass destruction, and its contribution to activities which undermine the Middle East peace process. It also includes the *fatwa* against British author Salman Rushdie and the bounty for his murder: a *fatwa* that symbolizes, in the minds of many Canadians, an intolerance that is all but incomprehensible, and the antithesis of values we hold dear.

To make matters more complicated, Iran seems determined to send all the wrong signals. The bounty associated with the *fatwa* against Salman Rushdie was doubled. Two Bahai religious leaders are threatened with execution for exercising their beliefs. Iran continues to support violent activities which undermine the Middle East peace process. Suspicions have deepened of Iranian support for terrorist incidents abroad, and of course German Courts concluded that Iranian authorities at the highest levels were implicated in the Mykonos affair.

Last year, Canada's Foreign Minister, Lloyd Axworthy, ordered a review and assessment of our policy towards Iran. The result was a sharpening of our policy, one that we now call "controlled engagement". Whereas in the past we criticized instances of Iranian behavior in such forums as United Nations and other venues, or pursued individual issues with Iranian authorities through our

Embassy, we have not addressed our concerns with the Iranian government globally. Under our policy of controlled engagement, we have advised the Iranians that there is no prospect for normalized relations unless and until they demonstrate a clear commitment to address our concerns on all the issues that I have mentioned.

That said, today the key issue remains: Where do we go from here? How do we effectively get Iran to change its behavior? In our view, isolation is not the answer. We believe, and, in my opinion, we will always believe that progress is possible only through engagement. No one should be surprised that Canadians take such a view. Our bilingual and multicultural federation exists because of our commitment to dialogue, to compromise, to an understanding of the other side. Similarly, we do not believe that the economic isolation of Iran will have the desired political effect. Indeed, if sanctions are called for, in our view, they must be multilateral; they should be UN sanctions.

Let me be clear that we have no objection if individual countries like the U.S. decide not to trade with Iran. However, we are firmly opposed to certain states attempting to impose unilaterally their trade restrictions on third parties through the extraterritorial application of their laws. In other words, the Iran-Libya Sanctions Act may be good domestic politics in the U.S., but from our perspective it is not a basis for an international consensus on how to deal with Iran. If anything, it impedes a consensus.

To conclude, for Canadians, Iran remains an enigma. It has such potential, and yet so many of its current policies are extremely troubling and threatening. We must work harder amongst our partners on how to approach Iran. We must be more creative in our dealings with that country. We must find mutually acceptable means to convince Iran to pursue its domestic, religious, and social agenda in a manner consistent with international norms, and to desist from activities which threaten international peace and stability. We are, in short, open to new ideas.

Before concluding, I should note that I did not raise the question of El Sayegh who currently is detained in Canada and who probably is on the minds of many here. He is detained pending a deportation hearing. Our authorities believe that we have overwhelming circumstantial evidence of complicity in Al Khobar. But beyond that, I really cannot comment, as the case is before the Courts, and it would not be my place to do so. And with that, thank you.

Iran and Bosnia-Herzegovina

Nedzib Sacirbey
Ambassador at Large, Bosnia Herzegovina

Usually the sons sit for their fathers, but I am sitting here for my son, Amy Mulamed Sacirby. There is some difference. I am a little bit older, and much heavier; while he speaks without an accent; I speak with an accent.

All Muslim nations are friends of Bosnia. The Iranian government supports Bosnia, and the Iranian people are friends of Bosnia. There is no government in any Muslim country that can refuse supporting Bosnia. Maybe we do have some problems in Tripoli, Libya, and in Baghdad, Iraq. Those countries have reservations about our government, our policy, and our country. However, when the well-being of Bosnia is at issue, Tehran, Tripoli, and Baghdad are united.

We very much appreciate and are grateful to the people of the U.S., its government, and both parties, Democrats and Republicans, because, as Senator Lieberman once stated, Bosnia has not become a partisan issue in this country. There would be no Bosnia today if there were no support from the United States of America.

On December 22, 1992, twenty-eight of the main Jewish organizations in the U.S. gathered in front of the Holocaust Museum, reading an open letter to President Bush and President-Elect Clinton, asking them to undertake military intervention to stop the bloodshed in Bosnia. The American-Jewish community was the first line of support for Bosniaís existence, and was a leader in protesting the genocide in the form of ethnic cleansing that was taking place in Bosnia.

Consequently, we do not differentiate among these three groups — American-Jewish community, United States of America, and Iran — all supported Bosnia. These are the facts. We appreciate what Iran's government did for us, we are grateful to the United States of America, and we recognize and express our thanks to the

American- Jewish community.

We in Bosnia have Muslims and Christians, Catholic and Greek Orthodox, and others. We have a Jewish community, too. Less than two weeks ago, at a conference in this city, one Rabbi stated that Sarajevo is the capitol of tolerance and multi-religious existence. The people who repeatedly state that we fight each other all the time, and have hated each other since we have been there, are simply ignorant. I am saying ignorant, not uninformed, because in using the term "ignorant", there is an element of condemnation, because such statements should be condemned since they are baseless.

In not a square mile but in one square kilometer in Sarajevo, we have mosques, synagogues, and churches of various Christian religions including the Greek Orthodox, Catholic and Evangelical Church. Many existed until the Communists expelled the Germans because of their collaboration with Hitler.

Our relations with Iran are of concern for some people. Our President goes to the mosque every Friday, as President Clinton goes to church every Sunday. We do believe that Muslims have rights to their religion, as do Christians or Jews.

When people talk about Judeo-Christian civilization and point of view, we feel that we are left out, regardless of the fact that historically and logically this is wrong. But there is something more that is wrong. Everything that is Islamic is considered as something that is the enemy. Definitely this is paranoid thinking. Good Muslims are to be tolerant. Since about the 14th Century, Christians have coexisted in Egypt with the Muslims; in 1492, Jews came to Sarajevo, escaping the Spanish Inquisition, and they have remained with us; the Greek Orthodox Church has been based in Constantinople. These examples, I believe, are proof that tolerance is something that is congruent with Islam.

However, we have reason to believe that intolerance exists against Islam and Muslims, and is frequently present in Christian circles. Please do not be offended, but give thought to this possibility . . . Am I wrong or am I right?

Something happened to us in Bosnia that really had not happened since the Holocaust. They tried to exterminate us. In order to further our extermination, I have to say, an arms embargo was enforced upon us, with one explanation ñ that if we were armed, there would be more killing.

We understood in a very simple way, that all of us would be killed if we did not have arms, because we would be unable to defend ourselves. We did not have war in Europe because of concern about what would happen to us if we attacked others, or about what the defense of the other side would do.

In 1993 and 1994 our existence was in question. Not existence as a country or as a state; but existence as human beings. Because our enemies were not against Bosnia and Herzegovina as a country; they were against Bosnians or Bosnian-Muslims. They were not wanted. Ethnic cleansing, rapes, concentration camps, killing, torturing — all of these were the tools used by the Serbs to eliminate us from the face of the earth.

These are the facts. And we are very much concerned as to why Europe did not act to stop this killing. Four years and a few days ago, at the opening of the Holocaust Museum not far from here, Elli Weizel cried, "Mr. President, something has to be done!" A sign of civilization is human solidarity. Our experience is that Europe was less civilized than it would like to believe, because it did allow our killing.

When Colonel North organized armament of Iranians, nobody said he was under the influence of Ayatollah Khomeini. When someone organized the armament of Bosnia so that we could defend ourselves, our existence and our life, it was believed that we had come under the influence of the Islamic Republic of Iran.

Iranians are Muslims. We are Muslims. I, myself, try to be a practicing Muslim. But my concept of Islam is different than the concept of some Iranians or of most Iranians, or of the concept that is promoted in Iran. Yes, we were recognized by Iran; we have diplomatic relations; we do have support. Iran sends us arms, sends us food, and gives us money.

Under our influence, they did have a trade agreement with Croatia, a country which is 95% Catholic.

We do not want to see ourselves as Iranian footsteps in Europe, because there will be paranoia, and we prefer to see the people mentally healthy. If policy is inspired by fantasy and false imagination, it definitely leads to paranoia. And paranoid leaders have committed a lot of wrong to mankind in general.

Shah Mohamad Rezah Pahalavi, the last Shah of Iran, visited Sarajevo and met with some Sarajevans. He was impressed that some people spoke fluent Persian. Yes, they did speak fluent Persian. Why? Because Persian, Turkish, and Arabic are, in some ways, the languages of Islamic culture, just as Latin became the language of Christianity. Many people forget that everything written by Maimonedes was in Arabic.

Some so-called religious texts were written in different languages — St. Augustine wrote in Latin, Maimonedes wrote in Arabic, and Jelalludin Rumi wrote in Farsi. Devoted Christians read the text of St. Augustine. Devoted Jews read the text of Maimonedes. Devoted Muslims read the text of Jelalludin Rumi.

It was the reason that there is a circle among Sufis in Bosnia, and a very small number speak Persian. If there were more people who do speak Persian, probably it would be better for our diversity. The main foreign language spoken in Bosnia at this time is not Arabic, is not Turkish, is not Persian, but is English. Next to English is German, and after that is French. Some time ago the main language was Russian.

We do have an Iranian Cultural Center in Sarajevo and have Iranians in Sarajevo. We visit the Iranian Cultural Center, and we open ourselves to Iranians. We do believe there is mutual influence. I know that there is no ideological influence of Iranians on us, yet I believe there is a lifestyle influence of Bosnians on Iranians.

We have one very simple approach. We do not try to recognize enemies. We try to create friends. We are not trying to act as someone who tries to find differences, but we are the people who try to find common grounds. It is our beginning. Otherwise we would not have dialogue at this time with the Serbs, or with the Croats.

Radovay Karazdic, who was my student, tried to justify our termination, saying that we are the footsteps of Iranians as they march on Europe. Sometimes he said that we are the footsteps of the Saudis on their march to Europe. Yes, we do have the support of the Saudis; we do have the support of Iranians, but not because we are pro-Saudis or pro-Iranians. We are pro-life and existence for Bosnians.

We do believe that the existence of Bosnia in Europe will

help Europeans understand Muslims; will help Muslims understand the West; and will be the bridge between the Middle East and the West. We do not want to say that we are most like the Middle East, but we fall somewhere in the middle. We want to see ourselves basically as human beings.

It is true that we Muslims go with the statement that Muslims are brothers. But there is a deep Islamic belief that all human beings are equal in creation. Consequently, all of us are part of the same humanity. If we are promoting this concept, the meanings of Shalom, or Salamaleykum, or peace, and good as Francisco de Assisi tried to promote, will be part of our coexistence, and building a better life on this planet, not just in Europe, will be the goal. But for us Bosnians, it means that we will survive and continue to exist as part of humanity. Thank you.

Questions and Answers

MS. JULIA NANAY (Petroleum Finance Company): Thank you for that very moving talk. Before we move on and open the floor to questions, I will summarize what some of the speakers have said.

I think that everyone agrees that there are human rights issues, that Iran sponsors terrorism, that there is a bounty on Salman Rushdie's head. But once all of this is taken into consideration, I think that what all of the panel members have said is that they have agreed to disagree with the United States on how to deal with Iran.

Russia is increasing both its trade and investment ties. The European Union may reassess how it goes about critical dialogue, but it is not likely to abandon it. The trade is too big between the EU and Iran, and the issue of oil imports is too large for the EU to give up on Iran. Canada is in a delicate situation right now because of the Saudi detainees. But Canada also does not support unilateral sanctions, nor Iran's isolation. And clearly Iran has been a friend of Bosnia.

So then, the EU says that Iran will not drive a wedge between itself and the U.S., but, on the other hand, there is definitely a wedge. So it seems to me that the U.S. will be left with unilateral sanctions, and that there will be a two-pronged critical dialogue going on. It will be between the countries represented here and Iran, and between the countries represented here and the United States.

And so the rest of the world is trying to decide how to find common ground with the United States. Although I do not know if this can be resolved, I question whether there is any chance that the EU may move in a different direction on this issue?

MR. STEFAN VAN-WERSCH (Embassy of the Netherlands; Current European Union President): What is a different direction? We have had, after the Mykonos case, two weeks of intense discussions among the Europeans, and not one country has come up with the idea of sanctions.

If you mean by another direction that the EU imposes economic sanctions, I would say that for the future, for the direct future, it is very unlikely that the EU will move into that direction.

If you mean by another direction, closer convergence with the United States, then, as I said, that development is on its way. What will come out of it, I am not sure. First, as I said, The EU will have to reformulate its own policy next week. After that, we will have the normal, regular, semi-annual discussions with the U.S. and Canada, by the way, on our policies towards Iran. You can be sure that during that meeting ñ which will be within two weeks — the issue of how to work together, have closer cooperation, and possibly convergence will, of course, be a very important point on the agenda.

But again, with regard to economic sanctions, there is nothing, there is no indication at all within the European Union that we are moving into that direction.

MS. JULIA NANAY (Petroleum Finance Company): One last question before I open the floor. On the issue of the World Trade Organization, do you see that, in the future, Europe would pursue the unilateral sanctions issue with the WTO more aggressively?

MR. STEFAN VAN-WERSCH (Embassy of the Netherlands; Current European Union President): We have done much to compromise and avoid a showdown on this issue with the United States, and to gain an "understanding". It is, however, certainly not excluded that ultimately we will go all the way to the WTO, primarily for the Helms-Burton Act. As I said before, we do not like it if our laws are being made in Washington. I would like to hear the outrage if it were the other way around. It is, on principle, wrong, that policies be made in this way. If one country decides to have sanctions, and it tries subsequently to force other countries to follow that policy, it is, in principle, unacceptable.

Of course we are willing to see what we can do. In order to get a waiver, we are working together with the Administration. But the principle will remain that we do not accept this way of cooperation, or rather, non-cooperation.

AUDIENCE: I have a question for Mr. Hughes and a question for Mr. Konarovsky. First, Mr. Hughes, the National Iran Oil Company has offices in Calgary, Alberta, and a company called Cala Naft, which is associated with it. They are purchasing U.S. oil field equipment in the U.S., and sending it on to Iran. My question is: Do you have re-export controls? Do you keep watch on this kind of trade? Do you have any controls on it?

For Mr. Konarovsky, *The Washington Times* has reported recently that Russia has been cooperating with the Islamic Republic to build, to transfer technology, for the SS-4 ballistic missiles, for S-300 air defense systems, and SA-18 air defense systems. My question is this. Does Russia currently have military technicians in Iran? If so, what are their particular fields of expertise?

MR. STUART HUGHES (The Canadian Embassy): A comment and response, if I may. The comment is that, with regard to Mr. Van–Wersch's remarks, which I endorse in many ways, we tend to lose sight of the fact that EU, Canada, and the United States may differ on the means that we pursue in wanting to see Iranian behavior changed. I do not think, Mr. Van–Wersch, that we differ particularly in the goal of seeing that behavior changed. This dialogue should emphasize the positive — that is, that we do share the same goals — it is the means that are in question.

With regard to the export of equipment which may be of U.S. origin, there are controls in Canada over the re-export of materials. Our basic policy is that we do not see Canada as a transshipment point for products coming from another country, or as a way of getting around the laws that may exist in the United States about the export of their products. So there are controls.

MR. MICHAEL KONAROVSKY (Russian Embassy): In reference to your question about SS-4 and S-300, I do not have any information about such supplies to Iran. Basically Russia is continuing to cooperate with Iranians on the basis of previous defense agreements signed in the late 1980's. There is understanding between the two presidents — between President Clinton and President Yeltsin — that after the pipeline is over, Russia will not sign such new agreements with Iranians. As for the second part of your question, about military experts, I do not know anything about it.

DR. DANIEL BRUMBERG (Georgetown University): I have a question for Ambassador Sacirbey. I want to say, first of all, that I applaud very much the point that you made, which is that the people of the former state of Yugoslavia have not hated each other for centuries. The American media did a good job of simplifying the culture and history of your country, and in promoting the erroneous view that somehow the product of the Yugoslavian Civil War was the product of ancient hatreds. It was the product, of course, of the manipulation of political leaders.

Having said that, are you not concerned that the presence of Iranians in Bosnia might lead to the effort of certain Iranians to manipulate religious traditions in your country away from the multi-religious, open view of religious tolerance that has been part of the history of Bosnia? We have numerous reports from Americans working on Eastern European affairs who have gone to Bosnia and have found, not so much in Sarajevo but in smaller towns, that where you have Iranian operatives working, they have intimidated the local populace, they have intimidated people in the press, and they have, in fact, attempted to change the practice and approach that has dominated the religious tolerance in your country. Are you not concerned by these reports? Or are they, in your opinion, exaggerated?

MR. NEDZIB SACIRBEY (Bosnia Herzegovina): Thank you for the question. You give me opportunity to clarify several things. There is no Iranian influence in Bosnia. There is the desire by Iran to have influence in Bosnia. Iranians did benefit from helping the Bosnians, because it improved their standing in the Islamic world. Sympathy for Bosnians in the Muslim world is high.

When President Izetbegovich met, with President Suharto, in October, 1992, President Suharto stated, "On the smallest island, in the last village, they collect money for help to Bosnia." When my friend, Serg from Bosnia, who works for the Library of Congress, went to Kenya a couple of months ago, one Massai fellow asked him, "Where are you from?" He said, "I am from Bosnia." His next question was, "Are you Muslim?" This means that Western journalists have helped make the world aware of the Bosnian cause and suffering.

Definitely the Iranians want to help U.S. in order to demonstrate so-called Muslim solidarity, and, at the same time, to increase their influence in the Muslim world. There are no Iranian troops there. The so-called Mujahideen, we did have them, around 600, were not Iranians; but they were from Afghanistan, Pakistan, Saudi Arabia, and everywhere. There is no really Iranian influence upon our government. There is no Iranian influence on our religious education or upon our religious community.

Do Iranians have the desire to influence us? I believe the answer is yes. About a year ago (in July) they provided an exhibit about Iranian culture and Islamic tradition. Many of us went to see it, because we would like to enrich our knowledge about Iran in general, and wanted to see what they had to show us. But I am sure that there is no ideological influence of Iran in Sarajevo, in any city, in any village, or in any mosque.

They are Shiite; we are Sunni-Hanafi. We have been under the influence of secular concepts for a long time. The secular concept does not mean that you can be free of religion in your heart and in your daily life. We must have the right, all of us, to practice our religion. But, at the same time, I add that, in Bosnia, someone who does not want to practice religion is free.

There is no definitely Iranian influence. I was asked in Montreal by one journalist, "In the past you did have so many mixed marriages. Now there are voices against them, and there is not any more". The Communist government encouraged mixed marriages. Our government tolerates, and more than tolerates mixed marriages, because law, civil law, allowed marriages between different religious and ethnic groups.

The Rabbis in this city and clergy in the churches speak against mixed marriages, saying that the best marriages are between two equals in faith and religion. You will find similar statements all over this planet. You will find such statement among our clergy in Bosnia, Muslims and Christians, too.

There are no cases in which a Muslim who was married to Christian kicked out his wife during this aggression, yet there are Christians who kicked their Muslim wives out during this time. We are proud that tolerance is part of our faith, and we will continue to have it and protect it.

AUDIENCE: My question has to do with your policy towards terrorism in general, not just Iranian-related terrorism. This morning we had a discussion of oppositionists who are violent towards the regimes back home. Do you include such people on your list of persons to be excluded? Persons to be somehow treated differently from others who are granted asylum in Europe?

Take, for example, the three Kurds who were killed in Berlin. Do we know anything about their background? They are called dissidents. Were they violent dissidents? Do we know anything about their previous behavior?

How do you handle people of that type? When you have a situation such as death squads operating in Spain against the Basques, how do you deal with that kind of phenomenon? Could you talk about how you deal with the problem of violent terrorism in general, not just as it relates to Iran?

MR. STEFAN VAN-WERSCH (Embassy of the Netherlands; Current European Union President): This is a totally different question, I would say; not one I expected.

In the first place, I think that it is very much up to the member state, where the situation occurs. Every member state has its own sovereignty in regard to these matters. Within the European Union, there is, of course, close cooperation on issues of this sort. There are even two special working groups on terrorism.

In accordance with the policy on asylum, it is quite clear, of course, that we always check to determine if there is a criminal background. Having a criminal background, including terrorist involvement, is, of course, clearly a reason for an exile to be denied asylum.

Cooperation in regard to both crime and terrorism, is increasing within the European Union. What started as an economic community, I would say, is now expanding its focus to include foreign policy and cooperation regarding matters of the interior, including crime. There is even closer cooperation of some member states, by now the majority, in regard to policies pertaining to visas and asylum.

So it is very intense by now, and it will evolve further. Within the Union, as you know, there are always some issues in regard to which member states say, "We want to keep our own sovereignty". But cases arise which make it absolutely clear that sticking to national sovereignty would not work. These are normally the examples that are being given for defending further coordination, further cooperation between the member states. Environment is one and crime is another one, since it is quite clear that borders do not exist for pollution, nor for criminals, nor for terrorists. About the three Kurds, I could not give you the precise information. You would have to ask my German colleague.

MS JULIA NANAY (Petroleum Finance Company): I have

one other question for Mr. Konarovsky. Just yesterday, I believe, Mrs. Albright made a statement regarding NATO expansion and Russiaís concern over the build up of military capabilities on the part of the countries that join NATO. Mrs. Albright said that the U.S. will stand very firmly in that regard, and will not give in to Russia's demands. If that is the case, do you see your military cooperation with Iran and China growing more aggressively to offset that position to your west?

MR. MICHAEL KONAROVSKY (Russian Embassy): No, frankly, I do not think so. First, you might remember that our cooperation with China began long before the Western Alliance announced intentions to expand NATO. Second, China has been, and will be, in any case, a very important neighbor for the Russian Federation. Under any circumstances, Russia will be much interested in expanding cooperation between our two nations, a fact that was affirmed a couple of days ago by President Yeltsin and China's President.

I am saying the same about Iran. Russia is against any kind of new divisions in the world, against any type of new alliances, military or political, in general. That is why we are not interested in having a new alliance against NATO, which, in our view, should not be expanded either. It is only speculation in the press, and probably, by freelance analysts, but Russia does not have such things in mind.

LUNCHEON ADDRESS
Oil in US-Iran Relations

Opening Remarks

Cyrus Tahmassebi (Chair)
President, Energy Trends, Inc.

My name is Cyrus Tahmassebi and I am the President of Energy Trends, Inc. I have the distinct pleasure and honor of introducing our luncheon speaker today. I have also been asked to make a few comments about some of the issues that are the subject of this conference.

As I said, I am honored to chair today's session. That honor stems from two things. First, it comes from the conference itself. I think the subject under discussion and the quality of the speakers make this a very interesting and useful forum. I am also honored because our luncheon speaker happens to be a very good friend of mine and our friendship actually goes back to something like 25 years ago.

This morning we heard a number of very interesting speeches about the political situation in the Middle East. As I was listening to these remarks, I noticed that a number of our speakers were quite emotional about their views and the political position they took concerning the Middle East in general, and Iran in particular. Let me tell you at the outset that I am not a political analyst. In fact, I do not consider myself to be anyone who knows anything about politics, particularly international politics. Basically, my expertise is in the field of energy, specifically in the oil and gas industries. My comments therefore, relate to those segments of this morning's discussion—and possibly what will be discussed this afternoon—oil and Iran.

In this morning's discussions we heard a number of comments about the U.S. sanctions against Iran, their effect on the Iranian oil and gas industries, and the long-term ramifications of the U.S. policy for world oil supply, etc. My view on this subject — parts of which were presented in a major seminar on sanctions here in Washington last year and subsequently were published by the Middle East Economic Survey — is that sanctions are of two types: 1) sanctions which have clear cut economic objectives with no overt or hidden political agenda; and 2) sanctions that are imposed on a country in order to exact political concessions.

In my opinion, sanctions with economic goals, lend themselves to an objective cost-and-benefit analysis. Since the objective is commercial, both the country imposing the sanction and the targeted country can look at the costs and benefits involved and can make a business-type decision. Normally, there is very little — if any — emotion involved in these analyses. As a result, sanctions of this type have a much better chance of accomplishing their objectives in a relatively short time — which often means that the parties involved reach a compromised solution to the issue or problems that triggered the sanctions.

Unfortunately, when it comes to sanctions imposed to achieve political objectives, the situation is dramatically different. Almost invariably, sanctions of this type are accompanied by a great deal of emotion, and neither side is ready to give much thought to the economic costs or benefits of such policies. As a result, sanctions with political objectives either completely fail to accomplish their objectives, or it might take years or even decades before even a compromised solution is reached. In the process, many innocent people are subjected to a very harsh and long punishment.

If you look at the Post World-War II era, I suppose the only sanction that has succeeded is the one that was imposed on the apartheid regime in South Africa. Other than that, if you look at other sanctions — for example sanctions against Cuba, Iraq, Iran, Libya — none of them have been successful. These sanctions have been almost a complete failure when applied unilaterally.

When sanctions focusing upon political objectives are applied, the sanctioning country is not ready to lift or compromise because of the emotions involved. The high commercial and economic cost of these sanctions unfortunately becomes an almost irrelevant issue. The targeted country, on the other hand, also is not ready to give in, simply because accepting the demands of the opposing party would be tantamount to a political capitulation. Such a political capitulation has the potential to reduce popular support for the government and undermine its stability much more than the hardships of the sanction itself. As a result, the government in the targeted country may actually harden its position and thus the sanction may drag on for decades with no compromise or solution in sight.

If you want to know about the impact of the U.S. sanctions on Iran, let me tell you about my own observations. I recently paid a visit to Iran, after some 17 years of being away. It appeared to me that the U.S. sanctions have created certain hardships for most people, but I want to tell you that most people have gotten used to these hardships. People are no longer awaiting an unknown abrupt change that could modify their standard of living or their life-style significantly — as was the case in the early years of Revolution. Most people seem to have accepted the *status quo* as a new *modus operandi* and are busy with their own daily activities.

I was amazed to see how different the Iran of today was from what I had seen in 1980. In the years after the Revolution, there was much anti-Western and anti-American sentiment. However, during my recent trip I did not see that. Frankly, this time I did not even see very many people talking about America or about American policy towards Iran, as was the case in the early years of the Revolution. People rarely ask a visitor coming from America what he thinks the U.S. government will do, for or against Iran. It is almost as if the U.S. policy towards Iran is irrelevant, or, at least, no longer as important as it was perceived to be by the general public only a few years ago.

In the West, we are given the impression that the U.S. sanctions are really hurting Iran and eventually will bring the regime to its knees. I certainly did not notice any indication of that. In a discussion about the Iranian economy, one individual told me that inflation is really hurting people, but he was quick to add that the rate of inflation in Iran is much lower than in most of its neighboring countries.

Let me stop here with those remarks, and introduce to you the luncheon speaker. As I mentioned, I have known Mr. Mossavar-Rahmani for almost 25 years. Back in Iran, I first got to know Mr. Mossavar-Rahmani when he was associated with an Iranian think-tank organization, engaging in energy-related research, and was writing columns for an English language newspaper. Later Mr. Mossavar-Rahmani worked for the Iranian government at very senior positions and, as you may have noticed from his biographical information, he also represented Iran in OPEC meetings.

He truly has a very unique background. He has been in

academia — at the Kennedy School at Harvard where he engaged in much energy-related research, seminars/conferences and teaching — and in a long and highly successful career in the energy industry, where he served as the President of Apache International. In addition to this unique professional background, what makes Mr. Mossavar-Rahmani even more qualified to address this gathering is the fact that the topic of this conference is Iran-US relations. He has lived in both of these countries for many years and is intimately familiar with the feelings of the people in both countries. With that introduction, ladies and gentlemen, it is my pleasure to introduce to you Mr. Bijan Mossavar-Rahmani.

Oil in U.S.-Iran Relations

Bijan Mossavar-Rahmani
Chairman, Mondoil Corporation

Dr. Tahmassebi, thank you. Ladies and gentlemen. I have been assigned an awkward and a difficult task this afternoon. Awkward because the luncheon speaker, positioned between long and intense morning and afternoon sessions, is expected, in part at least, to take a lighthearted approach to his topic. But there is nothing in U.S.-Iran relations, least of all oil, of which I can make light.

My task is made difficult by the fact that there are no U.S.-Iran relations, to speak of, and certainly, there is no oil in U.S.-Iran relations. No Iranian oil is purchased by U.S. companies, and no U.S. companies are active in Iran's oil sector in any meaningful way.

That there is no oil in this non-relationship is underscored by the fact that I am the only executive from the U.S. oil industry who is on the program of this conference. This would not have been the case in such a gathering 20 years ago, perhaps not even two years ago. And this will not be the case in future conferences held two years, or certainly 20 years, from now. So I am challenged in my task only by virtue of the timing of this meeting.

It has been said that wherever you dig in Iran, you either hit oil or uncover history, often both in the same place. I will therefore start with some oil facts, and a little bit of history.

The importance of oil in the US-Iran relations of the past, and again of the future, is driven by three things. One, Iran sits atop some of the world's largest tapped and untapped reservoirs of oil and of natural gas. This country's oil reserves are the second-largest in the world, after Saudi Arabia's, and its gas reserves are second-largest in the world after Russia's. Two, Iran sits a stone's throw – make that a day's drive or sail – from other countries that together possess over one-half of the world's oil reserves, and an irreplaceable portion of its daily production. Three, Iran sits astride the Persian Gulf, with a coastline longer than that of any other country along this body of water, through which about one-half of the world's traded oil moves. The tankers there are only a stone's throw away from Iran.

Also, in terms of the logistics of oil movements, Iran sits conveniently between billions of barrels and trillions of cubic feet of Azeri, Kazakh, and Turkmen oil and gas on the one hand, and the sea lanes of the Persian Gulf and access to the outside world on the other.

Most of you already know these facts. Still, they are worth repeating again and again and again. These facts were not lost on American policy makers in the 1950s, 1960s, or 1970s. In fact, obsession with Iran's importance in the global oil supply picture was in large part responsible for this country's role in overthrowing the government of Dr. Mohammad Mossadegh some 45 years ago. Many of you will recall that Mossadegh, who was *Time Magazine's* man of the year in 1951, and was a popularly-appointed Prime Minister of Iran, who nationalized Iran's oil, then owned, controlled, and operated by the predecessor company to today's British Petroleum. After nationalization, panicked and humiliated, its oil supplies and its profits threatened, London solicited Washington's aid in staging a coup d'etat to overthrow Mossadegh's government. . . and Washington obliged, in return for about one-half stake in Iran's oil for its own companies. The memory in Iran of that event in 1953 helped trigger the 1979 takeover of the American Embassy in Teheran, and the hostage crisis that ensued helped get us in the pickle we are in today.

No one, least of all me, is advocating a return to the oil relationship that existed in the 1950s, '60s or '70s. But to ignore the importance of Iran's oil is to do so at your own, and everyone else's, peril. For it is naive, even by Washington standards, to believe that Iran will not again be a key player in the global oil market some time after the turn of the century, regaining its previous production levels, and thus, its stature and significance in a world whose consumption levels continue to increase. On the other hand, it is wishful thinking, even by Tehran's standards, to believe that Iran's oil potential, particularly in the sphere of exploration and production, which is the sphere that really matters, can be realized fully, and in a reasonable time frame, without American technology, American capital, American entrepreneurial skills, and American oil management know-how.

This is self-evident to me, as one who has worked in, and is intimately familiar with, the oil industries of both countries. But as obvious as these realities are, and as critical as is the need to look beyond the current posturing and accusations and hostilities and threats and bruised egos and rhetoric on both sides, the big picture — that is, the longer-term view — is "held hostage" to last week's and last month's and last year's squabbles.

What needs to be done? How does each side work, essentially within the existing political, legal, and institutional constraints, to begin to put oil on the front, or at least on the side, burner? From the U.S. point of view, as we heard this morning, the Iran sanctions legislation does not permit direct investment by our industry in oil sector activities in Iran. However, the legislation has left a small, but not insignificant, opening: the participation of U.S. companies in arrangements with a swap or exchange of oil produced in neighboring land-locked countries — notably, the Central Asian Republics — for oil produced in Iran. In other words, if an American company produces oil from a field, say, in Azerbaijan, the swap mechanism would allow that oil to be delivered to an Iranian port on the Caspian Sea in return for the lifting of a like volume of Iranian oil in the Persian Gulf.

In such an exchange, the U.S. company gets to export its Azeri production to world markets, the government in Baku receives revenues from that transaction, Iran gets oil in the north, where it mostly consumes it, thereby saving the cost of transporting oil from the south of the country where it is produced, and the world oil market gets more barrels for more sources, enhancing security of supplies and helping keep prices in check. Everyone benefits, with the exception perhaps of Russia, which prefers to have all oil from the Caucusus exported through its territory, if at all.

Iran's economic gain from this transaction is marginal, basically consisting of the transportation savings accrued from not piping 50 or 100 or 200 thousand barrels a day up the length of the country. But even that gain will have to be shared with others involved in this transaction. There is no other benefit per se to the Iranian oil industry, other than engaging it in the formation of a regional oil supply and transportation infrastructure.

I happen to think this is a great idea, in no small part because I originated it in 1991, when wearing a different corporate hat, I was engaged in negotiations to develop a large off-shore oil field in Azerbaijan. Familiar as I was with Iranian oil transportation infrastructure, consumption patterns, and refining placements, and with no alternative export routes, it seemed that the cheapest, quickest, and easiest way to get oil out of the Caspian Sea was to conduct swaps with Iran.

I took this up to the highest levels of government in Azerbaijan, and in Iran. Both countries endorsed it enthusiastically. But the project, unfortunately, fell victim to changing political circumstances in the region and beyond. It is time to resurrect it.

Incidentally, some small volumes of oil have already started to be swapped with Kazakhstan, involving the Kazakh share of the Tengis oil field production. This experience initially has been an unhappy one, because Tengiz oil contains substantial amounts of mercaptans of sulfur, an impurity which has not been properly processed and removed and has thereby gummed up the Iranian refinery at Tabriz.

To the Iranian side, I offer a different proposal for jump-starting a re-engagement with the United States oil industry: improve the terms, the economic and operating terms, for participation in the countryís oil exploration and production sector.

When Iran initially and reluctantly cracked open the door to foreign participation in its oil sector several years ago, the terms on offer were unrealistically skinny from the point of view of the outside investors. Iran was offering projects with low and fixed rates of return — in the single digits, and no real upside potential. Nobody came — or at least nobody stayed. Too many other, far more attractive opportunities existed elsewhere in the world, as more and more countries scrambled to bid for the attention and the investment of the international oil industry in their own oil sectors.

Iran, therefore, missed a historic opportunity, in the early to mid-1990's, to bring in companies to develop a series of previously-discovered, but idle oil fields, particularly off-shore, or to explore for new ones. By the time Iran's expectations had become more realistic and reasonable and in tune with those of the rest of the world, that is, by the time the first deal was concluded with Conoco, it was too late. The United States slapped on sanctions, and the door was slammed shut.

About a dozen projects remain on offer since 1995. But despite some expressions of interest, the largest international oil companies have stayed away.

Iran needs to get aggressive, very aggressive, and offer terms that are highly competitive with those available elsewhere. That is, it should offer production-sharing contracts that allow companies to reap substantial rewards, if successful, to offset the risks — political and technical — inherent in this business.

Iran's requirements for outside capital are in the tens of billions of dollars. Iran has had no real exploration activity conducted for some 30 years, and its production technology, for the most part, is just as old. In the upstream — or exploration and production — arena, 30 years is many, many generations. To put this in perspective, the advances in exploration and production technology — that is, in three-dimensional seismic evaluation, directional drilling, computer hardware and software capability, off-shore drilling reach and platform design — the enhancements in these areas in the past five years have exceeded all the improvements of the previous 25 years. And again, Iran has had limited access even to the technology of those past 25 years, much less to the most recent advances.

Despite its long history of oil production, therefore, Iran is virgin territory, in oil terms, at least by the standards of 1997. Many international oil companies each drill more wells in a month, some in a week, than Iran drills in a year.

Iran has had some successes recently in developing limited local capability in the fabrication of off-shore platforms, for example, which have helped stabilize its combined off-shore and on-shore output in the range of 3.5 million barrels a day, where it has languished for years. But operations remain essentially hand-to-mouth. With proper application of technology, capital, and management, production can be increased by 50 percent in less than five years, and doubled in less than ten.

But that potential cannot be achieved without U.S. companies — the engine of the international oil industry. The U.S. companies have, in this regard, abdicated their role: sitting back while Congress and the Administration have slapped on sanctions, not only on Iran, but on Libya and Iraq — three countries which between them have hundreds of billions of barrels of oil at very low finding and production costs. These sanctions have been piled on in response not only to the political behavior and military posture of these countries, but were also seemingly necessitated by the mismanagement, by successive U.S. administrations, of the relationships with these countries.

The industry should take the lead in reversing this course, at least with respect to Iran, and the best way to engage the industry is to offer terms that we, the companies, cannot refuse. This is a card Iran has not yet played. Make the commercial terms attractive enough, and the companies will come, stampede-style, trampling the sanctions along the way.

I was in Iran recently to participate in an international energy conference, and made a similar point about the necessity of improving commercial terms in an effort to make Iran an attractive place to invest. I was asked by a senior Tehran official present at that meeting whether my speech contained a message from Washington. Well, of course, it did not. But it did contain a message from Houston and Tulsa and Dallas and the rest of the oil belt of America. Incidentally, in that speech I also called for the break-up of the Iranian governmentís monopoly of the energy sector. Deregulate, privatize, liberalize, globalize, I said.

I took on two particular issues. First, I noted that by unleashing competition by foreign and domestic companies, energy sector investments would become market-based, resulting in more efficient arrangements and greater and cheaper supply availability. Investment decisions, I noted, are still made in Iran, as they are made in many developing countries, by government ministries and state monopolies that are often inefficient, inflexible, and directed by non-commercial considerations.

Policy makers should get out of the way, I said. Let business do business. Allow the private sector, both domestic and foreign, to participate in all investments. Let commercial considerations dictate where and when and how much to invest.

On a favorite topic of long concern to me, I cited the example of a project that would not go ahead in Iran if investors had to invest their own moneys. That project is the construction in the southwest of two Russian nuclear power plants. The nuclear power project would never move forward in a country with so much gas, I noted, not based on Western technology, and certainly not based on older and unsafe Russian technology, if the investment decisions were made by private companies. I quote myself from that speech: "Let our Russian friends build reactors in Russia and sell electricity if they can compete with electricity generated by private companies in Iran using domestic gas. That is putting the market to work". I digress momentarily to note that it was the United States that planted the notion in Iranian minds in the 1970's that nuclear power was the way to go.

I made another point. "Do you think," I asked my Iranian audience, as I ask you here, "do you think the United States would have put on its current sanctions against oil investments if American companies were already operating in Iran? If Conoco or Exxon or Enron or Mobile or Mondoil, for example, were already well established and in place?" I think not.

Remove the obstacles to outside investment, I suggested. Encourage it. Offer wildly attractive terms. Commercial terms, not politically correct ones. For by insulating and separating investment decisions from domestic political considerations, you also insulate and protect your energy sector from international politics.

I winced as I listened to myself say those words in Iran that day. For that, I am afraid, is a lesson lost on us here in the United States, where foreign investment decisions and commercial interests are too often hostage to domestic political considerations, or at least, to domestic electoral prerogatives. Thank you.

Questions and Answers

DR. CYRUS TAHMASSEBI (Energy Trends, Inc.): Mr. Mossavar-Rahmani, thank you very much for that very interesting and insightful talk. I am sure there are a lot of questions to be asked. Yes, Dr. Sick.

DR. GARY SICK (Gulf 2000 Project, Columbia University): I enjoyed your talk very much, and I think it is really very insightful.

I wonder to what extent you — particularly as someone who watched this in the past — to what extent, curiously enough, is Iran really resuscitating the Shah's plans, and simply beginning to follow them almost blindly? I see this certainly in some of the activities that the Iranians are undertaking in the nuclear field, but also, I think their naval operations are very much a resuscitation of the Shah's plans. Even now, they are talking about and are sort of proud of the fact that Iran was there first with this idea, when its discussions really began with the Shah instead. I wonder if you see that as a factor, or whether it is just sheer coincidence that they are doing this.

MR. BIJAN MOSSAVAR-RAHMANI (Mondoil Corporation): There is some of that, and disturbingly so, from my point of view, with respect to the nuclear power program, where some of the same rhetoric is used to justify construction of nuclear power plants, which are totally unnecessary for Iran. It is not across the board, but I have been surprised to see how much of the same logic drives decisions in the energy sector today, and how much of the same language is used to support those decisions. It is almost as though they are reading the same script.

DR. CYRUS TAHMASSEBI (Energy Trends, Inc.): Let me just add a few words to Mr. Mossavar-Rahmani's comments. I worked for the National Iranian Gas Company (NIGC) from 1972 to early 1980, and was in charge of the feasibility study of numerous LNG or pipeline gas export projects. I actively participated in the negotiations concerning these projects and was instrumental in the signing of a number of these export projects. We thought they all were good projects for Iran, but, after the revolution, they received much criticism. Since the top guys had left the country, I was the only person left to respond to the critics. Almost daily committee meetings were held, during which the people instrumental in developing these projects were harshly attacked by some elements in the company. But now, as Mr. Mossavar-Rahmani just mentioned, things have changed a great deal. In fact, the conference at Kish Island was organized to attract foreign investment for a gas export project.

I think the only explanation for this change is that the early revolutionary fervor has been replaced with pragmatism, and the people in charge today are not the same people who were running things in the early years of the post-revolutionary period.

MS. JULIA NANAY (Petroleum Finance Company): Yes, I had a question, two questions, actually. One pertains to this issue of swaps through Iran from Azerbaijan. Assuming that American companies were to decide that they were cornered on the west, that they could not get out through Georgia, and they could not get out north through Chechnya; and presuming that in the AIOC currently two of those fields are supposedly in disputed waters. But let's say we got around all that. How much oil do you think could be swapped out? Are there the facilities in northern Iran? I do not know if the pipeline is there to receive them. How much could the refinery take?

My second question relates to the fact that I have heard that since there are not companies that are bidding on, for particularly the gas fields that do not have Condensate associated with them, like the Samman field, that the Iranians are determined to develop particularly South Pars, because the other side of South Pars is in Kutrah's waters. And then the Samman field, because it is also linked into Abu Dhabi's ABK field.

Could the Iranians, would they have the resources? Let's say that the Iranians convinced banks to lend them the money. Do the Iranian companies that are actually involved in some of these deals have the technicians to carry out the projects? Even though they may not have the technology, and, presuming they could get money from German banks for instance, could they go ahead and develop these projects without Western companies?

MR. BIJAN MOSSAVAR-RAHMANI (Mondoil Corporation): In response to the first question, which is the easier to answer, the Tabriz refineryís capacity is on the order of 200,000 barrels a day. The Tehran refinery is on the order of 250,000 or close to 300,000 barrels a day. So that gives you something like 450,000 – 500,000 barrels a day between those two refineries.

The existing south-north crude pipeline could be reversed. So Iran could take as much as a million barrels a day, with very little difficulty, if there were the capacity to barge the oil to the Iranian side of the Caspian Sea, but such capacity currently does not exist.

I would not advocate that Iran take that kind of volume, because then it would be vulnerable to whatever happened in the Caspian area. Nor would I advocate that the Caspian countries exclusively ship their oil to Iran. The Iranian option is one of several alternatives. It would not be prudent for either side to rely on any one particular route, but the potential, the logistical capacity, the infrastructure in Iran is substantial.

With respect to technicians in Iran, there are of course good technicians in the country. But it takes more than a technician to make these projects happen. Again, you need capital. You need technology. You need management capability. None of those exist in Iran on the scale necessary to do much more than maintain oil production at about its current level.

Again, as Dr. John Lichtblau mentioned this morning, off-shore production is rising; on-shore production is down. It is the on-shore arena where Iran really has massive potential, but for which the country has not been prepared, politically, to open up, at least at this time. One of the advantages of off-shore fields is that the foreign technicians, too, can stay off shore. And it was not clear that the American companies or other companies wanted to have large numbers of their people on shore, deep in the heart of Iran.

So while Iran can maintain production at about the current level, it does not have the range of capabilities required to boost production to the levels to which I referred earlier.

MS. JULIA NANAY (Petroleum Finance Company): What about their foreign exchange? The Iranians say that they have enough money now, particularly with high oil prices last year. Could they dedicate some of that money to develop those two fields in particular on their own?

MR. BIJAN MOSSAVAR-RAHMANI (Mondoil Corporation): Sure, they could, at least to some extent. I do not know how many billions would be available, one or two or three. I noted they need tens and tens of billions to do this. But why spend it? The oil industry is one in which you can attract outside investment. So what you want to do is to harness whatever foreign exchange reserves you have to those target projects and activities for which foreign interest does not exist. With Iran's oil, if they opened the floodgates, and if we the industry stampeded, we could take with us tens of billions of dollars and free up Iran's foreign exchange for other uses.

MS. JULIA NANAY (Petroleum Finance Company): Do you think U.S. companies would do this in spite of the sanctions ? That they would stampede in, even if, let's say, the terms were incredible?

MR. BIJAN MOSSAVAR-RAHMANI (Mondoil Corporation): Oh, absolutely. When I first started negotiating with them, they were talking about rates of return at two or three percent. We explained that was crazy. By the time Conoco came around, I expect the percentage allowable returns were in the twenties.

You offer rates of return of 50 percent, and watch those sanctions go.

AUDIENCE: As a Washington lobbyist for Conoco and the oil industry, I wish I could say that I have experienced anything like the degree of influence that you seem to suggest that we do! But I appreciate your suggestion, because certainly if the Iranians did improve the terms, it would demonstrably enhance the focus and pressure to lift the sanctions.

In regard to sanctions pertaining to Iraq, we noticed that the U.S. government's interpretation of those sanctions is much more strict than interpretations of the Europeans, Asians and Russians. We are kind of afraid that by the time those sanctions come off there, the crumbs will be left. What would make you think that in Iran it would be any different?

MR. BIJAN MOSSAVAR-RAHMANI (Mondoil Corporation): In terms of what is left after the others take the pickings?

AUDIENCE: Exactly.

MR. BIJAN MOSSAVAR-RAHMANI (Mondoil Corporation): Iran's potential is massive. First, I do not want to make light of sanctions. Remember what the Chinese tried to do with relatively modest sums in the last presidential election. Then consider the billions and billions and billions of dollars at stake in the oil and gas business. You can move mountains, certainly Senators and Congressmen, with a fraction of that kind of cash.

The Iranians have not really focused on that, because they

have been caught up with their own rhetoric — Islamic rates of return, keep out the foreigners, that sort of talk — that has prevented them from really playing the oil card, which I believe they can play. So no one has come to the party. Total came, but it has now stepped back, and brought the Malaysians in to invest the real money. That is a very small project in terms of the opportunities in Iran, of which there are plenty. These are not opportunities the Malaysians can handle or even the French. The international exploration and production business is about the American oil companies. I do not think the others can fully tap those areas, nor would it be desirable from Iran's point of view to have these more expensive and less efficient companies coming in to run the whole show.

DR. CYRUS TAHMASSEBI (Energy Trends, Inc.): Is it not also true, Mr. Mossavar-Rahmani, that some of the technology and drilling is actually proprietary? That the U.S. companies are the only ones who probably have it?

MR. BIJAN MOSSAVAR-RAHMANI (Mondoil Corporation): Some of it is, but less and less so, because a lot of the advances and technology that I spoke of were not really initiated by the oil companies. They were initiated in Silicon Valley. The advances in the computer hardware and software capabilities came from beyond the oil industry. You can purchase those, but you still need the people to come in and manage and implement them. Iran has access to neither the technology nor the people right now.

AUDIENCE: I wanted to follow up on the notion of Iran offering very attractive rates of return to American companies. Do you see any realistic likelihood of that happening? Do you also see the equally necessary willingness to allow those high rates of return to continue long enough actually to recover the investments, and take account of the risks, as any American company would want — not just for the political risks in Iran, but also for the political risks in the U.S.?

MR. BIJAN MOSSAVAR-RAHMANI (Mondoil Corporation): Obviously, this is the hurdle that Iran needs to cross. Again, they crossed the hurdle from two to three percent rates of return, to 20 to 25 percent rates of return once. If you send me to sell, and no one is going to buy, then you have to keep adjusting your price to generate the interest. Whether or not Iran will play this card, I cannot say.

My strong feeling is that if they made the terms attractive

enough, certainly the non-Americans would start going into Iran. That would put a lot of pressure on the American companies, and through the American companies, on the U.S. government and the U.S. Congress to remove the sanctions, or somehow adapt the sanctions to allow those investments to take place. Other countries have done this before, and oil and money speak very, very loudly.

Now, the other point that you mentioned is a more difficult one. What do you do if the Iranians offer 50 percent rates of return, and say that everyone is welcome? Then, once all the companies have gone, the Iranians switch the rate of return back down to 20 percent or 15 percent or 10 percent. Now, that is a case of nationalization. This becomes a different kind of a problem, and companies should adjust their own risk profiles and take the appropriate steps to cover themselves in anticipation of such an event. Obviously, there are no guarantees that terms, once offered, will remain in place.

The country where terms have changed the most, in a fiscal sense, is the U.S.. This is the place where, over time, oil companies have been nationalized more often than anywhere else in the world. It is done by changing the rules under which you play. So this is something the oil industry has lived with for 100 years, and knows how to deal with, in terms of managing its portfolio and spreading its risks. I am not terribly concerned about the ability of the oil companies to adapt.

DR. TOM STAUFFER: Mr. Mossavar-Rahmani, I am absolutely intrigued by your argument that the presence of profitable American oil companies would preclude sanctions. That really is quite edifying for all of us who have been watching recent developments, because you have conclusively proved that the sanctions in Libya do not exist. For us here, that means one down, and only two more sets to go.

DR. CYRUS TAHMASSEBI (Energy Trends, Inc.): Well, I think, as I mentioned at the beginning, I was expecting this to be a very interesting session, and it seems like it has been. Let's thank our speaker, and move on with the program.

KEYNOTE SPEECH
A View from the U.S. State Department

Introductory Remarks

Hooshang Amirahmadi
Professor and Director Middle Eastern Studies
Rutgers University

It is a pleasure and honor for me to present to you Mr. Robert S. Deutsch, Director of Northern Gulf Affairs of the State Department, who will deliver the keynote speech.

Because the subject is very important, and the time is quite short, I will be brief. I wish, however, to point out that, first, Mr. Deutsch's biographical information is in your folders; and second, that as a foreign service officer, Mr. Deutsch has had, and continues to have, a distinguished career.

He has served the U.S.' economic and political interests in many parts of the world: Europe, Africa, and elsewhere, including the Middle East, of course. His outstanding efforts have been widely recognized, and this recognition has extended to his colleagues in the State Department who have awarded him the Superior Honor Award.

We are fortunate to have Mr. Deutsch address our group and tell us about the U.S. policy in the wake of the Mykonos verdict.

A View from the U.S. State Department

Robert S. Deutsch
Director of Northern Gulf Affairs
United States Department of State

Thank you, Dr. Amirahmadi for the introduction. I am happy to be here this afternoon, among so many familiar faces.

Somehow, the topic of Iran always seems to attract a large and very interested group. We are frequently asked to speak about Iran, but what we say does not change that much, or, at least it has not changed much over the last two years or more, because, to a great extent, what Iran does has not changed that much over the last four years. Therefore, while there is a healthy debate over policies, there is not that much that can be changed in terms of those policies.

Iran continues to pose a significant threat in a region where the United States has vital national interests. Over the last four years its policies have not changed for the better. The Iranian regime still seeks to project its regional influence through a conventional military build-up, and through the development of weapons of mass destruction and their means of delivery.

We are particularly concerned by Iran's continued pursuit of nuclear technologies, chemical and biological weapons and production materials for them, and missile technology. Iran's acquisition of ever-more-sophisticated missile technology from North Korea and China presents an increasing threat to our friends, and to our military presence in the Gulf.

Iran's threat is not limited to the military arena. Iran seeks to expand its influence by promoting violence around the world. Iran has used terror to disrupt the Middle East peace process. It seeks to gain influence through disaffected elements in neighboring countries, and by promoting subversion of neighboring governments, and it has supported terrorist activity from South America to the Far East.

Iran's use of terror recognizes neither allies nor frontiers, age nor sex, religion nor ethnicity. Not even Iran's own people are protected from its violence. Iran's human rights record is one of the worst in the world. Its ethnic and religious minorities and its women regularly feel the lash of Iran's repressive system. Its disrespect for the right of free expression is vividly demonstrated by the regime's public offer of money for the murder of another country's citizen, Salman Rushdie, because of what he wrote. Others who dare to stand for freedom of ideas, like the Iranian writer Faraj Sarkuhi, also suffer for their courage.

Iranian oppositionists face less public, but equally dire, threats. Two weeks ago the German Court found that the assassination of four Iranian Kurds at the Mykonos Restaurant in Berlin was ordered by the highest level of the Iranian government. These murders were part of a broad pattern of state murder that has claimed the lives of some 50 Iranian dissidents since 1990. What more tangible proof could I offer of Iran's willingness to use terror and violence in pursuit of state goals?

Meanwhile, the Al Khobar investigation continues. We have not yet reached any conclusions. If the evidence demonstrates involvement by Iran or any other state, we will take appropriate action to ensure that justice prevails.

What is the goal of U.S. policy on Iran? We seek to change Iranian behavior through economic and political pressure, while directly limiting Iranian capabilities. In the interim, we seek to constrain the resources that enable Iran to pursue activities that threaten us and our allies.

Our previous speaker suggested that, if there were free investment, Iran would have available to it billions of additional dollars that could be used for other purposes that would not be funded by international capital. I can only shudder at what some of those purposes might well be.

We seek neither to permanently isolate Iran, nor to overthrow the Iranian regime. We do not object to the Islamic government. We do want Iran to abandon those policies which have made it an international pariah.

Our approach includes non-proliferation and counter-terrorism efforts, combined with economic and political pressure. To combat global terrorism, we are developing a common agenda with our European allies based on the P-8 counter-terrorism measures. On non-proliferation, current legislation enables the U.S.

to pursue its objectives towards Iran; international cooperation curtails, although it does not eliminate, Iran's access to the technology and equipment that is necessary for proliferation.

Our current sanctions laws allow, help us to deter the access which terrorist countries such as Iran have to nuclear, chemical, and biological weapons, missile equipment and technology, advanced conventional weapons, and lethal military assistance. However, some governments continue to assist Iran with its missile program and its programs related to weapons of mass destruction. That is why we have combined non-proliferation efforts with economic and political pressure.

We seek to demonstrate to Iran that these policies will not only fail, but will be very costly to its economic and political interests, and to the well-being of its people. By targeting weaknesses in Iran's economy, particularly its need for technology and foreign capital, our unilateral efforts have limited Iran's policy options. For example, Iran has had difficulty attracting foreign investment for its oil industry due to the threat of U.S. sanctions. Iran must therefore choose between funding development projects and funding the very policies to which we object.

I have outlined our response to the threat posed by Iran. Now I would like to discuss how we think we could be more effective. We would be much more successful if we had a larger cooperative effort. We do have significant cooperative efforts with other major developed countries in Europe and Asia, on issues related to counter-terrorism. We have other joint programs, joint efforts related to the array of issues pertaining to non-proliferation, and ranging from chemical and biological weapons conventions to a non-proliferation treaty.

But we believe that we need to move further along with our allies, to use our common political and economic clout to have a real impact on Iranian behavior. We have pressed our allies to adopt such an approach, and to restrict Iran's access to foreign capital and technology. We seek a coordinated, multilateral response that imposes clear consequences on Iran for its choices.

What would a successful common approach look like? Well, the steps taken on April 10th by the EU, the recall of ambassadors and suspension of the critical dialogue, expulsion of certain Iranian intelligence operatives, are solid initial steps. A common strategy that brings us closer together would have even greater impact. It would make clear to Iran that support for terrorist groups is unacceptable, period. We must be perfectly clear on that point. No support for terrorism, for any reason, at any time, in any country. We must take an equally firm stand on proliferation of weapons of mass destruction. While the world community is working to reduce and eliminate these horrible weapons, we cannot remain silent while Iran develops its capabilities.

The Europeans have said that they will meet April 29th to consider additional measures. We hope that the EU's decision will move our approaches closer together by including measures that impose a tangible cost on Iran. We want to create an impetus for Iran to change its behavior.

What do I mean by meaningful change? Well, I do not mean dialogue for its own sake. Efforts to engage Iran have not achieved any notable successes. Dialogue has not stopped assassinations in Europe. It has not ended Iranian support for terrorism. It has not stopped Iran's use of its embassies to coordinate arms procurement and terrorist action. Dialogue has not even succeeded in lifting the threat against Salman Rushdie. States that have engaged in dialogue with Iran have not received immunity from terrorism, nor have they influenced Iran to change.

Iran's revolution continues to evolve. Periodically, internal voices are raised to criticize the regime's internal and external policies, and to put at risk Iran's own development and stability. Unfortunately, these voices are not being given a serious opportunity for expression in next month's presidential election. The candidates in that election share a common investment in the status quo and its unacceptable policies.

As long as Tehran continues to seek to project Iranian power, violence, and terror in a way that threatens our interests and international stability, the U.S. will work to isolate Iran and to limit that threat. We will use all the tools at our disposal to protect our friends and our interests, responding forcefully to Iranian actions.

We call on our allies to join us in applying a real cost to Iran for its policies. We hope that U.S. leadership and the growing realization on the part of European nations that Iran's murderous behavior is unacceptable will lead us to work more closely together.

We are confident that the terrorist policies of the Iranian regime will not prevail, and that the Iranian people will force the Revolution to evolve and yield a regime that respects international standards of behavior and acts in the interests of all Iranians. Thank you.

QUESTIONS AND ANSWERS

DR. HOOSHANG AMIRAHMADI (Rutgers University): Mr. Deutsch, you began your presentation by saying that U.S. policy has not changed over the last four years because Iran's behavior has not changed. How many years will the policy remain in place, if Iranís behavior remains as such? Forever? In other words, the question is, which should change first, the behavior or the policy? If the policy is not changing the behavior, and is ineffective, why should it be continued?

MR. ROBERT S. DEUTSCH (Northern Gulf Affairs, Department of State): Well, as I suggested in my presentation, we do believe that the policy, while it may not change behavior, does serve to constrain the resources that are available to Iran. Iran has declared much, much broader intentions in terms of its military development, its military procurement and its military programs, than it has been able to realize. On the one hand, this has been due to the constraints placed on Iran by that part of the policy which has a fairly broad acceptance and which limits sales of military goods and technology to Iran. On the other hand, Iran has not had the economic resources to achieve its military objectives.

So, even if we do not succeed in achieving the goal of changing Iranís behavior through our policies, we do believe that those policies have enabled us to have a significant impact by limiting some of Iranís programs, particularly the military ones, that are of the greatest threat.

HENRY PRECHT (former Country Director for Iran, State Department): You spoke about dialogue. Dialogue is not linear. Have we made any efforts at dialogue?

MR. ROBERT S. DEUTSCH (Northern Gulf Affairs, Department of State): Well, when I talk about no results from dialogue, I would refer to the results attained by all of those countries who claim to be practicing a policy of engagement and dialogue in order to effect the behavior that we jointly pursue.

We have an open offer to the Iranians. We are prepared for

dialogue with an authorized representative of the Iranian regime, at any time. There are no preconditions, other than that, to avoid the experience of the mid-eighties, it be made clear to us that the Iranian representative is fully authorized. The Iranians know the appropriate channel through which that authorization should be communicated to us.

If such dialogue were to take place, we would be prepared for secret talks, although we would have to admit, publicly, that dialogue was taking place. From our point of view, we would want to have the full range of issues that concern us laid on the table.

HENRY PRECHT (former Country Director for Iran, State Department): I do not know why you would want a dialogue with a country that you depict in such terrible terms. In fact, I do not know why we would ever want to have anything to do with such a vile regime. I wonder if you could discuss, briefly, necessarily, some of the values or interests that we might share with Iran, if somehow miraculously that country were to fulfill all your conditions. What is it about Iran that would call us back again? Why do we not just simply write Iran off entirely if there are no redeeming virtues in that country? I have heard none listed by you today. Is there nothing there that attracts us? Has the revolutionary regime achieved nothing that we admire? Is there no basis for shared respect in the future? What is there of a positive nature?

MR. ROBERT S. DEUTSCH (Northern Gulf Affairs, Department of State): Iran has a long and storied history, it has a strategic geographic location, and it has lots of oil.

HENRY PRECHT (former Country Director for Iran, State Department): Its President is stepping down voluntarily. Can you name any other President in the Middle East who has done that?

MR. ROBERT S. DEUTSCH (Northern Gulf Affairs, Department of State): I could name another one, but you would not like the name I came up with.

HENRY PRECHT (former Country Director for Iran, State Department): Right. The Iranians have achieved higher levels of literacy than countries that we aid, such as Egypt, have they not? They have greater opportunities for women than other friendly countries in the area. Do these things count for nothing in the American equation?

MR. ROBERT S. DEUTSCH (Northern Gulf Affairs, Department of State): Not when the country in question is pursuing efforts that directly threaten our people, our interests, our friends. Certainly those are elements that we would seek to assist and promote in other countries.

MR. DON DeMARINO (US-Arab Chamber of Commerce): I am just recovering from this morning's threat briefing from AIPAC [American-Israeli Public Affairs Committee]! I am making sure my bomb shelter is in good shape. The Halle-Bopp Comet strikes again here!

I am just recovering from this morning's threat briefing on Iran by AIPAC. Without much in the way of factual support, AIPAC has been very good at putting out glossy brochures about Iran's military program, and some other things that I find curious.

Our colleagues at AIPAC shared with us an interesting statement: that Iran was on the march. I am curious whether you concur with some of the rhetoric-enhancing and inflammatory statements, or whether you feel that perhaps there is a middle ground here. Because, as a prerequisite for any kind of dialogue, it would seem that the most important thing is to lower the level of the rhetoric.

Do you agree with the position that Iran is on the march to cut a swath through the Middle East? Or do you really feel that perhaps there is a lower level of concern?

MR. ROBERT S. DEUTSCH (Northern Gulf Affairs, Department of State): I would not want to suggest that Iran is on the march, nor would I want to suggest that there is reason to feel complacent. I can certainly assure you that when I travel in the region to visit my friends in Northern Iraq, I am concerned about Iranian activities; I am concerned about Iranian MOO (Mobilization of the Oppressed Organization) and IRGC (Islamic Revolution Guard Corps) agents and what they might be plotting against me, personally, as well as what they might be plotting against U.S. facilities in the region, in Northern Iraq, in the Gulf and Turkey, and further afield. I am concerned about what they might be up to in terms of their activities in the Gulf, working against governments that are friendly to us. But I do not, I do not want to paint a picture that suggests that we are without resources, or on the run, or that somehow Iran has the long impetus of history behind it. I would agree with you that excessive rhetoric is not useful in dealing with Iran.

MR. ROSCOE SUDDARTH (Middle East Institute):   Mr. Deutsch, I wonder if you would describe for us what you anticipate happening in the next few weeks, in terms of the elections and the new governance that will come into being. Would you discuss the internal political situation in Iran, as it is now and as it is likely to be after the elections.

In describing the Iranian government, you presented a kind of monolith; but, based upon my discussions with many others, it sounds as if there could be two governments, and there are perhaps more, several factions operating. Could you give us a bit of clarification in regard to that situation?

MR. ROBERT S. DEUTSCH (Northern Gulf Affairs, Department of State): I certainly would agree with you that the Iranian system is not monolithic. However it is ruled by an elite group, clerics mostly, with support from the bazaar. This limits the real opportunities of governance to those within a certain range of opinions.

There are major differences among them. In our view, they tend to be mostly focused on internal matters. I think you would find some of the greatest divergence on issues such as the previous speaker raised — deregulation, privatization, returning some of the opportunities to the private sector.

In regard to the elections, it has been fairly clear for some time that, although there is still considerable competition, it is most probable that victory will be achieved by Nateq Nuri, who represents the militant, traditionalist school. No? Am I wrong? The more pragmatist wing, represented by Rafsanjani and Khatami, is likely to have a good bit of influence yet, to remain in the circle, and to be consulted. The Iranian system is not monolithic, but when it comes to military programs, when it comes to support for terrorism, there does not seem to be a significant difference among the political groups.

MR. MOHSEN SHOAR (Conoco): You just made a remark that the U.S. government is willing to talk to Iran; there is an offer on the table. During an interview with Mike Wallace, President Rafsanjani basically said that the Iranians are willing to talk to U.S. government officials, with no preconditions. Why has the U.S. government not made a public statement similar to what you are offering to Iran now?

MR. ROBERT S. DEUTSCH (Northern Gulf Affairs, Department of State): We have stated that — I do not know what you mean by "why has there not been a public statement." The position on dialogue has been stated repeatedly by U.S. government officials, at all levels, from the President on down.

MR. MOHSEN SHOAR (Conoco): Well, Iran made the offer to engage in dialogue, but there has been no counter statement from the US.

MR. ROBERT S. DEUTSCH (Northern Gulf Affairs, Department of State): If President Rafsanjani and the Iranian government are serious about it, they know how to get in touch with us.

NORA BOUSTANY (*Washington Post*): One thing that bothers me about our policy not evolving is that it seems we have learned nothing about the policies of exclusion and what they make people do. When others are excluded, they make sure that their presence is felt. We have learned that with the Iraqis, and with the Islamists in Algeria.

What is it going to take for this government to engage in a dialogue, as was suggested this morning, that will have checks and balances, rewards and punishments, but within a policy of inclusion?

MR. ROBERT S. DEUTSCH (Northern Gulf Affairs, Department of State): If you are suggesting that we make a unilateral change in our policies, I am not sure what the benefit would be. If the United States were to go hat in hand to Iran and say, "Okay, we desperately want a dialogue, be included," . . . I can assure you that, if anything, such an action would have a negative effect.

AUDIENCE: As I listened to you, I realized why it is that we are in the pickle that we are. You speak about the readiness of the Administration to have a dialogue, and about there being an offer on the table since the time of President Bush. And this gentleman makes reference to President Rafsanjani's comment that he is ready to talk. It sounds to me like President Clinton ought to learn some Farsi, and Mr. Rafsanjani ought to learn some English, and maybe they will come to a common language in which they can dialogue.

The issues to which you and the gentleman from AIPAC made reference suggest to me that it is not the behavior that you are seeking to change; rather, it is the nature of the country that you are seeking to change. It is not that you are trying to change the behavior, but rather, you want to alter the strategic necessities in the country that more or less transcend the political structure.

Now, I am appalled that throughout this entire day, only Mr. Mossavar-Rahmani's remarks contain some solutions. Yet everyone is talking about problems, problems, problems, problems. One would expect people occupying positions such as yours to be more imaginative, and a little bit more willing to take the initiative.

MR. ROBERT S. DEUTSCH (Northern Gulf Affairs, Department of State): I have heard many statements that suggest that the problem is the fact that there is no dialogue. Dialogue to produce what? Dialogue for what purpose? Dialogue is not an answer. Both sides must have the desire for change, to change the basis of the confrontation, of the problem.

We do not pose a threat to the existence of Iran. We do not pose a threat to the existence of Iran's friends and allies. We do not use murder as a weapon of the state. We are attempting to limit the threat created by a country whose behaviors are outside of the norms of the whole world, of the rest of the world — and whose behaviors are deemed unacceptable by the rest of the world — I do not see why the great solution to this is as simple as having the U.S. start talking to this country, with its hat in its hand.

AUDIENCE: Mr. Deutsch, as you know, next Tuesday the EU is having a meeting and will be discussing whether to continue critical dialogue with Iran or whether to abandon it. I would like to know your view on that, and what you expect to be the outcome of that important European Union meeting.

MR. ROBERT S. DEUTSCH (Northern Gulf Affairs, Department of State): I am going to refrain from making any estimates about what our European colleagues are going to decide next Tuesday. I do not think our European colleague did that this morning either.

But the question is not whether to cut off the critical dialogue or not. The question has to do with taking serious measures that will demonstrate to Iran that the international community, the world's body politic, is concerned about its behavior; and that the international communityís response to a country that feels free to threaten our interests and murder our people in our countries will not be determined simply by the dollar signs that Iran can sort of dangle out in front of our noses.

AUDIENCE: In 1993, NSC advisor Anthony Lake, wrote an article in Foreign Affairs, in which he offered dialogue with an authoritative person or body in Iran; as I recall, Robert Pelletreau again said something of the sort last fall when he was in the UAE. Now, the real question is, what were the official reactions of the Iranian government? Beyond those public statements, did anyone actually follow up on the statements of Anthony Lake or Robert Pelletreau?

MR. ROBERT S. DEUTSCH (Northern Gulf Affairs, Department of State): Well, I am not going to surmise about whatever private communications there are. Suffice it to say that they have not taken up the offer of dialogue.

AUDIENCE: Did they make any official responses?

MR. ROBERT S. DEUTSCH (Northern Gulf Affairs, Department of State): I am not going to get into whatever private exchanges there may be.

AUDIENCE: But public ones? Were there any public responses?

MR. ROBERT S. DEUTSCH (Northern Gulf Affairs, Department of State): There may have been some response in the press, but nothing significant, nothing that would engage a dialogue.

MR. SIAMAK NAMAZI (Rutgers University): I am no apologist for this Islamic Republic, and I cannot begin to tell you how it has affected my life personally. But when you stand up here and you say the U.S. has never posed a threat to the existence of Iran, and I know that Congress passes bills and officially gives money to overthrow the Islamic Republic, my Iranian side burns.

MR. ROBERT S. DEUTSCH (Northern Gulf Affairs, Department of State): How do you know that?

MR. SIAMAK NAMAZI (Rutgers University): How do you not know that?

MR. ROBERT S. DEUTSCH (Northern Gulf Affairs, Department of State): Are you saying that the U.S. Congress has passed a bill that proposes to overthrow the Islamic Republic?

MR. SIAMAK NAMAZI (Rutgers University): Are you telling me that there has never been support for groups like the Mujahedeen, the MKO?

MR. ROBERT S. DEUTSCH (Northern Gulf Affairs, Department of State): We have no contact with the Mujahedeen or the MKO. We consider it a terrorist organization.

AUDIENCE: Talk about the $20 million.

MR. ROBERT S. DEUTSCH (Northern Gulf Affairs, Department of State): What $20 million?

AUDIENCE: The Newt Gingrich thing. The Appropriations Bill, two years ago. Along with the statement that the government in Iran should be overthrown.

MR. ROBERT S. DEUTSCH (Northern Gulf Affairs, Department of State): Mr. Gingrich said that; but that is not U.S. government policy.

MR. SIAMAK NAMAZI (Rutgers University): When the Congress discusses this, how can I go around criticizing people in Iran for their stand on the U.S.? If the Iranian Parliament, if the Iranian Majlis sat around and said, "We want to pass money to overthrow the American government," what would be the reaction here? It is very difficult for me, it really is.

DR. HOOSHANG AMIRAHMADI (Rutgers University): The questions just raised are from my students. These are young Iranians who are as American as any of us, and they really are burning inside. That was the main point of my talk this morning, that as Iranian-Americans with a fragile identity, we would love to see America and Iran get together again. That is actually the reason for the reaction you hear, that is the real issue for most of Iranian-Americans.

DR. CYRUS TAHMASSEBI (Energy Trends, Inc.): You just said that Gingrich's statement was not the U.S. position, and it may be true. Let us apply this same logic to an Iranian example. For instance, I know that the official Iranian leaders have been saying that the idea of killing Salman Rushdie is not the Iranian position. It was not the position of the government. This is brought up every time I go to any of these conferences. So how would you explain that? Also, I have one more question: What will happen to the gas pipeline to Turkey?

MR. ROBERT S. DEUTSCH (Northern Gulf Affairs, Department of State): Well, we do not allow people in the United States to organize bounties to commit murder. The *fatwa* was declared by Ayatollah Khomeini, who was the supreme leader of Iran.

The *Bonyads*, yes, you can sort of try and distance them from the government, but they are all part of the same circle. The heads of the *Bonyads* are appointed by the leader. If the Iranian regime, if the Iranian government, decided it wanted to end the existence of the bounty, they could do it. It is not a uniquely private entity.

What is going to happen to the pipeline? I think you would probably have to ask the government of Turkey what it is going to do about the pipeline. We have communicated our concerns to Turkeyís government in regard to the revenues that it would provide to Iran and how this income might be used. We have explained to them how it might relate to our domestic legislation, and we have ongoing discussions with Turkey about what their intentions are.

PANEL III:
REGIONAL PERSPECTIVES

Opening Remarks

David E. Long (Panel Chair)
Middle East Specialist and Retired Foreign Service Officer

Dr. Amirahmadi asked me to say just a few words at the beginning to set the stage for discussing the Gulf region, and specifically, to comment upon the Arab States of the Gulf and the Arabian Peninsula. In so doing, I thought it might be interesting, and perhaps would shake up a few people, to compare and contrast the Arabian — basically the GCC — view of Iran with the United States' view of Iran, and to explore how differences in viewpoint interplay with policy in the Gulf. Despite close and friendly relations, the U.S. and Gulf viewpoints diverge considerably. The United States is a superpower and far away; the GCC is comprised of small states, and the superpower in the Gulf is Iran.

Thus, one can arrive at some fascinating contrasts. First of all, despite the demonization of Iran by our government and by many private citizens in this country, the animosity toward Iran in America really is not terribly deep. Earlier this month, I was a refugee of the blizzard in Rapid City, South Dakota. I checked into my hotel on a Friday night, and was not able to leave until Monday morning. Weather conditions were so bad during that time that neither guests nor staff could leave the hotel, and we got to know each other far better than we ever wanted.

During the three days of enforced South Dakota hospitality, I thought it would be fun to see what the attitudes of my fellow inmates were about various issues, particularly about Iran and the Gulf. As you can imagine, few had any strong views at all, but such as they had, there was not really much animosity expressed toward the Islamic Fundamentalists, or toward "satanic" Iran, nor were any of the other assumed popular American views of the region expressed. The others at the hotel were mildly curious, probably because I was there to answer their questions, but were not greatly worked up one way or another. Thus despite all the U.S. efforts to demonize Iran, it appears that anti-Iranian feeling does not run very deep.

Let us compare this to the Gulf. In the Peninsula, animosities are both deep and of long standing. I was struck by a statement this morning that animosities were not historical in the Balkans, which seemed to belie everything I learned in college about the Balkan problem in the 19th century, and indeed the Middle Ages. But nevertheless, the same cannot be said about the Peninsula. There, deep ideological, religious, ethnic, and national differences have been extant for centuries and transcend the official views of the regimes in that part of the world.

I am reminded of an example in the late 1960's, when the Shah visited Saudi Arabia to patch up a serious rift caused by Iran's seizure of an Aramco oil rig. The event took place at a time when the two countries were supposed to be close allies. While the two countries were attempting to paper over their differences, a glimpse was caught of a senior Saudi, just behind the Shah during a visit to Mecca, making a gesture that indicated "Shiia" in less than complimentary terms. I am sure the gesture was made out of mischief rather than malice, but it certainly illustrated how deep animosities between Arabs and Persians go. In contrast, American animosity toward Iran pales in comparison.

That said however, it is fascinating how the two sets of perceptions have played out in policy terms. For example, in the 1970s the Gulf Arabs were very nervous about the U.S. two-pillar policy, because we were trying to put them in bed with the Iranians against a common communist threat; they were very loath to be that close to Iran, common interest not withstanding.

The U.S.' views toward Iran have totally changed since the Iranian Revolution. We demonize Iran and we want the Gulf Arabs to do likewise. The fascinating thing, however, is that even though Gulf Arab animosity toward Iran is much deeper than ours, they are not willing to demonize Iran as we want them to do. On the contrary, they are far more willing than we are for dialogue with Iran, and in fact, they do dialogue with Tehran.

The lesson from this appears pretty clear to me. Despite deep and age-old animosities toward Iran, the Gulf Arabs nevertheless realize that the two peoples, as neighbors, will have to share the same space for eternity, and the Arabs are thus far more pragmatic than we when it comes to dialogue. Despite squirming in

Washington, that is probably a good thing.

There is a second lesson. Iran, despite its demonizing the United States, the Gulf Arabs, and any other fancied foe, is equally pragmatic. If and when Iran believes it is in its interest to behave according to international norms, it will do so. There is no reason, therefore, to worry about not encouraging Iranian moderates. When Iranians decide to be moderate, they will be. This is a lesson the Gulf Arabs know well, and is why they will not give away the store to promote friendship or confrontation. In the meantime, the Gulf Arabs see the Iranian threat as very real. They realize that they are very small and that Iran is very big militarily. They are afraid of the Iranians, or else they would not have us around. But, with all of their fears, they are still ready for dialogue.

Let me conclude with one last thought. With all that dialogue that the Gulf Arabs are willing to have, and with all the lack of dialogue that we insist upon, our strained relations with Iran have been pretty similar. Strategically, I think Iran and the Gulf Arabs are miles apart, or, if I may say so, a great gulf apart, and will probably remain so for the foreseeable future. So one must ask, as Mr. Deutsch did earlier, what good is dialogue if there is not an underlying desire to reach a mutually acceptable compromise. The Gulf Arab position, I believe, is that despite no basis for strategic compromise, it is possible through dialogue with Iran to achieve some limited tactical cooperation with Iran; and if some tactical cooperation can be achieved, I say all the better.

Now, with those happy words, let me give the floor to the panelists.

Israel and Europe in U.S.-Iran Relations

Geoffrey Kemp
Nixon Center for Peace and Freedom

One of the few advantages of talking in the afternoon is that many of the key points have already been made, so one can engage in editorial comments at this point in the day. There is a lot of consensus in this room. Everyone agrees that Iran is important and everyone agrees that there are elements of the Iranian regime's behavior that are obnoxious and have got to change.

The debate is about methods. The term "dialogue" has come up during every single panel. I would like to reinforce a point that Dr. David Long made because it is a very important one. Dialogue without any fundamental structural change in the position of the people who are participants in the dialogue does not guarantee anything.

For example, when the U.S. finally agreed to talk to the PLO, it was because of the significant change in the PLO's stated policies towards Israel. Today you can see that a dialogue between Israel and the Palestinian authority has not led to a lasting peace, and that there are thousands of extraordinarily complicated issues still to be resolved. The U.S. was engaged in dialogue with the Soviet Union for years and years during the Cold War. We had diplomatic relations, cultural exchanges, you name it. It did not fundamentally change the nature of the relationship, the issues that divided us, and the military preparations that everyone took in event of the worst case scenario. So do not let us raise our expectations too high if the United States and Iran eventually enter into a dialogue.

I would like to make two points in the twelve minutes I have left. The first is that there are two critical components to U.S. policy and its relations with the outside world that are going to influence the future. First is the relationship with Israel, and, in turn, its linkage to the peace process. Second is the U.S.' relationship with Europe, and how we respond, given Mykonos, and what may be coming up in the weeks ahead.

Until there is either a breakthrough in the Arab-Israeli peace process or a fundamental reappraisal by Iran of its interests in supporting Hamas and Hezbollah, I believe there will be little basic change in the United States Congress' support of tough policies towards Iran. Or, for that matter, in the support of such policies by other sectors of the country. So I do not want to talk a great deal further about the Middle East peace process, except that it is clearly a critical element influencing American policy.

The other dimension is the European one. This morning we had a representative from the EU here, who I thought rather brilliantly dealt with the very complicated fact that he is representing 15 countries who have tried to reach common ground on a series of very complicated foreign policy issues, including Iran.

The reality, of course, is that, while there is an EU position which we must take seriously, the key countries that we are talking about here are Germany, Britain, France, and Italy. If there were to be significant change in the policies of these four countries, that would carry enormous sway in Brussels.

It seems to me, that we are at a very interesting point in time, because there will be meetings; on April 29th, and the G-7 meeting in Colorado in June, where the key Europeans will be present as well as the Japanese. These will be occasions for reassessing the U.S. policy in conjunction with our allies. Furthermore, in the interim there will be an election in Iran, which may or may not bring about some willingness to change policies.

Before I discuss these details, I must first comment upon the issue which seems to have been avoided. This morning Dr. Cordesman very briefly mentioned the Khobar Towers evidence. We do not know as yet what evidence the Saudis are going to provide the FBI; certainly the public does not know about it. The fact of the matter is that this is going to be the seminal event in determining the nature of this debate, if indeed the evidence points very strongly to an Iranian involvement. Even for those who would like to see a new policy towards Iran, who believe the current policy is not working — and I am one of those — even for those who accept the idea that we need to think about change in policy, the reality is that if the evidence is strong, the U.S. will have to respond, and will have to respond very, very strongly.

The debate is about how this will happen. Will it be a military response? An economic response? A political response? A unilateral response? One with our allies, or one through the UN? All of these options are going to be debated.

In my view, the key here is Saudi Arabia, because the Saudis are the ones who are going to make the decision as to whether they will provide us with all the evidence. If they decide not to, then we will not have incontrovertible evidence. It is suggestive to me, from statements the Secretary of Defense has made recently, that we do not have that evidence at this point in time.

But, assuming that we do, I would make two further assumptions. One, that it would mean the Saudis want us to know it, and two, they would probably expect us to do something pretty drastic. The military options are clearly there. The Administration is prepared for massive military response, anything less than that will be very counterproductive and will not be supported by very many people.

A more open question and one that we should certainly consider is whether or not evidence that would be strong enough for our purposes would be enough to convince our European allies to be more assertive than they are likely to be over Mykonos.

China and Russia, of course, play important roles. One option for the Administration would be to take the issue to New York and try to get a Security Council resolution passed condemning Iran. Then the question would arise as to whether there would be any teeth to such a resolution, and what would we do if there were a veto, which would be likely if the use of force were advocated. I think China and Russia would probably veto such action.

Would that be bad for us, or would it mean we had taken the high ground and that we could then go to the Europeans and try to intensify pressure? This comes back to the basic point that we must address. What are the methods that are likely to succeed? After all, what we are talking about here is changing very specific behavior patterns of the Iranian government.

My instinct tells me that in the absence of conclusive evidence on Khobar Towers, the Mykonos case alone is not going to be enough to persuade the Europeans to look to economic sanctions, as Mr. Deutsch suggested earlier this afternoon.

The other day I was in an extremely interesting meeting wherein U.S.-German relations and Iran were being discussed.

Someone said, "Well, what would it really take for Germany, beyond Mykonos, to change its policy to include economic sanctions?" The conclusion was that it would probably take a move to assassinate Salman Rushdie literally on the doorsteps of Helmut Kohl's house, before the Germans would contemplate economic sanctions. I think there is great opposition to economic sanctions within the EU.

I am much more inclined to think that the one area where the Europeans are prepared to do more, in conjunction with the United States, is in the political and psychological arena. There has been little discussion of this today, but my sense is that the Iranian regime is not insensitive to where it stands, vis-à-vis the European Union. While Iran might show a very tough bravado when dealing specifically with Germany, it might be more responsive were the entire European Union and Japan more supportive of tightened political and psychological pressures on the regime.

Now, whether this would have the desired effect is questionable. This gets back to the point made by Nora Boustany: if you isolate a regime and try to keep it out, it will use unpleasant methods to get back in. That is a very basic issue that I do not think we have resolved today, and it is doubtful that we will.

Our policy needs reappraisal. I think we need to work more closely with the Europeans, and in my opinion, the best approach would be that of the good cop/bad cop. Let's be quite clear about what this approach means. It involves an agreed-upon script. Both cops must agree on what the outcome should be. The bad cop has to be prepared to adhere to certain rules of behavior, and the good cop has to be prepared to draw his gun as a last resort. The question then becomes, can we establish a series of benchmarks for Iranian behavior upon which both the United States and Europe can agree, and which will be put to the test?

I think there is absolutely no doubt in the minds of anyone that it is the United States that really holds most of the sticks and most of the carrots. Clearly, the U.S.' carrots are enormous, as discussed throughout the day. We have much more to offer Iran than vice versa, even though I do not discount Iran's importance.

The question is then, would Iran's behavior change more under the current circumstances in which disagreements between the U.S. and its allies are prevalent and which I believe the regime exploits, or, would greater change result from a combined approach that does not require the Europeans to engage in economic sanctions to which they will not adhere anyway. My belief is that the latter would be a step forward and that is the most we can probably expect in the short run.

Arab-Iranian Relations

Hisham Melhem
*Correspondent, As-Safir, Al-Qabas, and Radio Monte Carlo,
and Television Commentator*

Let me start by saying there is no uniform Arab approach to Iran. There are different, and at times contradictory, Arab policies towards Iran, which, in turn, has no uniform policy towards the Arab world even though in recent years it has attempted to improve its relations with the Arab States across the board, with mixed results. If I had to generalize, I would say that many Arabs are ambivalent about Iran, but I would not hearken back to the theories of deep animosity or deep Arab-Persian hatred. While those are significant factors that one should not ignore, the general attitude is one of ambivalence.

In our collective Arab memory, Iran, or rather Persia, occupies a special place, given the historical, cultural, and political tensions between the two sides, and given the tremendous contributions of Persians to Islamic civilization. At times, there has been a great deal of productive cooperation between Arabs and Persians, and this is something which should be kept in mind, also.

The relationship definitely has not been one-dimensional, as some of the propaganda emanating from Baghdad or Tehran would have us believe. It was, is, and will continue to be complex and multi-faceted, with an inherent element of tension, even during periods of cooperation. That has been true in regard to the relationship between Iran and Syria, between Iran and the Sudan, and between Iran and "its adversaries" in the Arab world.

In modern times, Arab-Iranian relations have been heavily influenced by outside powers. Since World War II, they were particularly affected by U.S. policy and by the conflict with the Soviet Union. Before the Revolution, Iran and the conservative Arab States in the Gulf dealt with each other under an umbrella of American-led security in the Gulf. The U.S. at times managed to arbitrate and mediate tensions between its various conservative friends in the Gulf.

In the 1950s Iran and Iraq were members of the anti-Soviet Baghdad Pact. By the 1980s both states were engaged in the deadliest and longest war, conventional war, in the Middle East in this century.

In the 1960s, Iran's close alliance with the United States over oil issues and security in the Gulf, and a close relationship between Iran and Israel contributed to tensions between Iran and Egypt when it was under Gamal Abdal Nasser, as well as between Iran and other so-called radical Arab States. Tension with Egypt paralleled tension between Washington and Cairo, in the sixties.

Naturally, the Shah, with Western blessing, would lend his support to those conservative Arab States who were at loggerheads with Egypt. When President Sadat allied Egypt with the United States in the 1970s, the Egyptian-Iranian relationship became friendlier.

Many Arabs, particularly the Iraqis, were alarmed by the Shah's aggressive policies in the 1970s. It was imperial Iran, not revolutionary Iran, that laid claim to Bahrain. It was imperial Iran that projected military power into Oman in the early 1970s, and it was imperial Iran, probably with a wink from the West, that occupied the three islands claimed by the United Arab Emirates.

The Iranian Revolution led to dramatic changes in Iranian-Arab relations. The Revolution was welcomed by a number of Arab States: Syria, Algeria, South Yemen, and the PLO. It was supported by many intellectuals, including many secularist intellectuals. This is because of the deep resentment against the Shah's policy. This is also because of the Iranian Revolution's support for the Palestinians. The Revolution, however, alarmed Iraq and the conservative Gulf states, not to mention Jordan and Morocco. The support for the Revolution among ordinary Arabs may have accelerated Saddam Hussein's decision to invade Iran in September of 1980.

The Revolution's hostility to hereditary rule, its challenge to the status quo, and opposition to the U.S., and its support for Islamic movements and calls for Islamic solidarity across the board were seen by the conservative Gulf states and Iraq as attempts at exporting the Revolution. And they were not entirely wrong. The takeover of the Grand Mosque in Mecca in 1979 and the Shiite rioting in the eastern part of the kingdom confirmed the earlier fears about revolutionary Iran.

The divisions among the Arabs on how to deal with revolutionary Iran continued during the first phase of the Iran-Iraq War; i.e., the period between 1980 and 1982, when the Iranians liberated their territories. Ironically, Islamic Iran received the support of socialist Algeria, Bathist Syria, Marxist South Yemen, and Libya, and also, the PLO, to a certain extent. Egypt, Morocco, Jordan, and the Gulf States supported Iraq politically, financially, and logistically.

Support for Iran on the governmental level, as well as on the popular level, began to diminish rapidly as a result of the excesses of the Revolution, and after it became clear that Iran — or, I should say, Ayatollah Khomeini — would not end the war against Iraq until the fall of Saddam Hussein and the liberation of Iranian territory. The war, however, forced Iran to pursue a more pragmatic policy towards the Arab States. This did not put an end to Iranian political, moral, and probably financial support for Islamist movements in the Arab world, or military support for Hezbollah in Lebanon.

In the 1980s Saudi Arabia, Kuwait, Bahrain, and others accused Iran of instigating violence in their territories, although the Iranians vehemently denied this. Notwithstanding the revolutionary rhetoric and Islamic ideology, Iran's foreign policy, even during the reign of Ayatollah Khomeini, was driven by *raison d'etat*, and not by revolutionary ideals. It was the *raison d'etat* that convinced Iran to ignore Syria's crackdown on its violent Islamist opposition, in 1982. It was *raison d'etat* and enlightened self-interest that led Iran to abstain from any serious act of support against the Iraqi Shia during the uprising against Saddam's regime in 1991. After Iraq's invasion of Kuwait, Iran cleverly maintained a neutral posture, enabling it to enhance its image in the Gulf and benefit from Iraq's strategic blunder.

The initial fear in the Arab world that the Iranian Revolution will become an emulated model has been greatly exaggerated. Iran's limited success with Hezbollah in Lebanon is unusual, and mainly due to the historical role the Shia of Lebanon played in spreading the faith in Iran in the 16th Century, added to the current socioeconomic conditions in Lebanon. Iranian influence in Lebanon is a function of the continuing conflict with Israel, and it depends a great deal on Syrian sufferance. No serious political leader in Lebanon today, in 1997, talks about establishing an Islamic Republic in Lebanon. Not since the mid 1980s has there been much talk along these lines. No serious leader of Hezbollah mentions this, even in background meetings.

Even the Islamist regime in Sudan does not consider Iran a source of inspiration. Although the two states — the two embattled regimes, I should say — do cooperate in many areas.

In recent years, Israel, Egypt, Algeria, Saudi Arabia, and Bahrain have found it convenient to accuse Iran of supporting Islamist groups violently opposed to their governments. They do not want to admit that the opposition is home-grown, and would have been active, regardless of Iran. In addition, Iran, for a variety of sectarian and doctrinal issues, has been unable to develop close relationships with the largest Islamic-Sunni movements in the Arab world, be they the Muslim Brotherhood in Egypt, the Salvation Front in Algeria, or Al Nahda in Tunisia.

Today's Arab relations with Iran cover the full spectrum. There is the usual tense, precarious relationship with Baghdad, and the cold, suspicious relationship with the Saudis and others in the Gulf. There are the close economic ties that exist between Iran and Dubai of the United Arab Emirates, notwithstanding the conflict over the three islands, and there are the good, solid political, economic and cooperative military relationships with both the Sudan and Syria.

Now, let me say a few words about some key Arab states.

Iraq and Iran: In regard to these two states, let me say that the Shat-tal-Arab is not only a physical divide between the two countries, but it is also a cultural divide, regardless of the fact that Shiites live on both sides of that divide.

There are many areas of dispute between the two states that would lead me to believe that tension will remain between them for a long time to come. Controversies include issues involving border disputes, the state of the prisoners of war, as well as support for opposition groups within each state. These two countries, if I could use an existential term, are doomed to live in a state of tension for a long time to come.

Saudi Arabia and Iran: It could be argued that attempts at full normalization will continue between Saudi Arabia and Iran, although in a lackadaisical fashion. This could change dramatically if it is determined that Iran was involved in the Al-Khobar bombing.

Now, there are two aspects which must be kept in mind. The

first has to do with whether or not it can be determined that Iran was involved, and if there is a smoking gun. This is very difficult, if not impossible to determine. On the other hand, and probably more importantly, if there is, in fact, a smoking gun, the question would be, will the Saudis be willing to assert this publicly, and allow the situation to unfold to its logical conclusion; i.e., American retaliatory action against Iran. I would argue that the Saudis will not do that, although it would be difficult to say this with certainty. I do not think the Saudis would like to see the Americans attack Iran. The Saudis do not trust the idea that the Americans can really change the government in Iran; or, the Saudis would say that the Americans would do to Iran what they did to Libya in the 1980s, and that Saudi Arabia would have to live with this colossus of 65 million people across the Gulf.

When we talk about Saudi Arabia, the other thing to bear in mind is the fact that the Saudis themselves — people in government, in the bureaucracy, in intellectual circles— are very concerned with this high American military profile in the Gulf. They see it, as they should, as becoming a source of tension in and of itself. Dual containment cannot be maintained, in the way the Americans would like, without that large military presence in the area, which is becoming a source of problem.

Sudan and Iran: Since the December 1992 visit by President Rafsanjani to Khartoum, there has been growing cooperation between the two states. They are considered pariah regimes by their neighbors — definitely by the U.S. — and they do cooperate militarily and economically. This is not neccessarily a case of Islamic solidarity; this is mainly a state-to-state relationship. In fact, Sudan needs Iran more than Iran needs Sudan, but, of course, the Iranians would not mind to have a foothold in Africa, in a country neighboring Egypt and across the Red Sea from Saudi Arabia.

Syria and Iran: These two have an extremely complex relationship; it is a beautiful marriage of convenience. Syria and Iran have a solid relationship, driven by *raison d'etat* and devoid of any illusions. The two sides know each other very well. Their relationship is described by both Presidents Assad and Rafsanjani as "strategic ties, a strategic relationship." Each state needs the other to balance the Turks and the Iraqis, and they share a common interest in getting the Israelis out of South Lebanon. This is a relationship that survived the two Gulf wars, and has been a constant, predictable feature in Middle East politics since 1979.

The differences which Iran and Syria have had over the islands in the Gulf and over Lebanon (Hezbollah), are not likely to lead to any serious rupture between these two states, because they have no illusions about each other, and they need each other. Both of them make political and not ideological calculations.

Let me make a few more comments about Iran's position regarding the Arab-Israeli peace process. Tehran's opposition to the Arab-Israeli peace process has been much vaunted, especially in Washington and in Israel. I would argue that a just and comprehensive Arab-Israeli peace would not threaten vital Iranian interests. Furthermore, Iran's support for Hezbollah and Hamas, in and of itself, does not thwart or reverse the peace process, if it is a genuine process.

However, Iranian leaders are guilty of speaking with many tongues. One can cite statements by Iranian President Ali Akbar Rafsanjani in which he denounced the peace process while at the same time he stated that Iran could live with it. That is an Iranian problem.

The rhetoric against the U.S.-sponsored peace process serves to bolster the regime's shaky revolutionary credentials. Even so, it is very doubtful that Iran would seriously risk its national security interests to uphold the rhetoric.

This is also why Iran is not likely to challenge a Syrian-Israeli peace agreement, since Syria will not accept any settlement that does not lead to Israel's total withdrawal from Syrian and Lebanese territories. The terms of a peace treaty between Lebanon and Israel would lead to the disarmament of Hezbollah, an outcome which Iran would have to accept because it values its multifaceted ties with Damascus, and because Hezbollah is already a well-established political party in Lebanon. Finally, let me say that regardless of all the descriptions of exaggerated tension between Arabs and Iranians, most informed Arabs realize that, within our region, any influence Iran enjoys today, or is likely to enjoy in the future, is a function of its size, location, history, culture, and economic potential; it is not a result of its revolutionary appeal.

DR.. DAVID E. LONG (Middle East Specialist; Retired Foreign Service Officer): Thank you, Mr. Melhem. I just want to make a very brief comment. Both you and I made reference to animosity. I actually did not mention it to say that it drives policy; quite the opposite. I said that despite the fact that there is more animosity in the Gulf, in regard to Iran animosity drives Gulf policy less than it does in the U.S., I believe, where the animosity is shallow. It is, to me, another one of those paradoxes.

Regional Implications of US-Iran Relations

Hassan Askari Rizvi
Pakistan Chair, Southern East Asia Institute
Columbia University

The problems in Iran-U.S. relations are quite understandable. Both countries have reasons to doubt each other as both have often worked against each other. There are strong psychological barriers between the two countries, which go back to the last phase of the Revolution and events that occurred immediately thereafter. These barriers have caused a serious communication problem, and created much distrust between the two governments.

The distrust is reinforced by the specific problems which currently exist between the two countries. During lunchtime, Mr. Deutsch talked about some of the American complaints; if you talk to some Iranian official, he also will give you a catalog of Iranian complaints against the United States. The U.S. and Iran have divergent perspectives on regional and international issues. So, when you put all these factors together, the situation becomes very difficult, a situation where each views the other with overblown fears, which are fed by super-heated propaganda and rhetoric.

What does this mean for the region? What are the implications of the strained U.S.-Iran relationship for the region? Because of the time constraint, I will address those implications briefly, providing more detailed discussion of the most significant concerns. Towards that end, I will make a few suggestions for the improvement of the environment in the region.

There are five major implications of the US-Iran confrontation for the Gulf region:

- The present-day regional security system is based on unrealistic assumptions, and involves very costly strategies on the part of the United States.
- There is a strong tension in the region because of this relationship, which has made it very difficult to develop a meaningful security dialogue within the region. A

country like Pakistan, which has traditionally maintained very cordial and friendly relations with Iran, has problems with Iran from time to time because of this relationship.
* The Afghan issue has become more complex, and its solution is more difficult now than was the case in the past. The American relationship with Iran plays a role in it.
* The great game in Central Asia is turning sharp,especially on oil and gas.
* Dialogue amongst the Muslim states has also been affected by the adverse relationship between U.S. and Iran. The development of a consensus on social and economic issues and on security matters has become extremely difficult because of this relationship.

Now, in regard to the first issue which I raised, the issue of Gulf security or the regional security, the present arrangement is based on three basic assumptions: 1) there is a need to contain Iran and Iraq; 2) Iran and radical Islam are the major threats to stability in the region, i.e., the Gulf and South Asia; 3) a very strong American presence is needed in order to protect and advance American interests in that area.

Such a security framework leaves very little room for regional or intraregional dialogue, and is based on the negative assumption of containment. It involves very high cost for the United States. The security system is based on the vast strength of an extraregional power i.e., the United States. A regional security system that does not involve dialogue within the region, will always be a precarious and weak arrangement. No viable regional security system can be developed without a dialogue amongst the states located in the region concerned.

The countries like Saudi Arabia and Iran have an uneasy relationship, and problems crop up periodically in the relations between Iran and Pakistan. Periodically, every few years, Pakistan has to reassure Iran that it will not allow its territory to be used as a staging ground for American military operations against Iran. The otherwise close relationship between Iran and Pakistan is marred by the tension that exists between Iran and the United States.

Iran has often adopted policies to get out of its isolationist situation, and has endeavored to create its own grouping, which may not be sympathetic to the U.S. interest in the region. Iran has talked about regional cooperation involving China and India, as both are unsympathetic to the U.S.. Although Iran has attempted to involve Pakistan in this arrangement, Pakistan has been reluctant to join the Iranian-sponsored regional security arrangement due to its relationship with India, and also, Pakistan wants to avoid the push-and-pulls of the U.S.-Iran conflict.

In my opinion, the U.S. attributes too much to the Iranian Revolution as far as the Islamic movements are concerned. Sometimes, by listening to American comments, one could be left with the impression that some Ayatollahs sitting in Tehran are masterminding everything, controlling the switchboard for all movements in the Muslim world.

I think that, in order to understand the Islamic movements, two basic things must be kept in mind. Islamic movements are not monolithic, but rather, they are very diverse and fan out in different directions. Secondly, where the Islamic movement has gained a foothold in other countries, this has been due primarily to factors found within the domestic context of each and every one of those countries. It is the failure of the secular order to ensure political participation and socioeconomic justice. Poverty, underdevelopment, and similar factors have given these Islamic groups an opportunity to project an alternate socioeconomic model. This is the root cause. It is readily evident upon examination of the role of these movements in Egypt and Algeria, as compared to that within Pakistan. But, I will not get into the details of why that role is different in Pakistan.

So, if the state becomes antagonistic toward Islam, and yet it (the state) is unable to provide socioeconomic justice, then the Islamic movement will develop and flourish. There may be a connection between Iran and Islamic movements. In certain cases, there are. But these movements would be there, even if there were no Islamic Iran, because the root causes of these movements are essentially domestic.

The rise of the Taleban in Afghanistan, and especially its control of the Western region, has ignited Iranian fears of encirclement. The Iranians feel that this Taleban orthodox Islamic group, which is pro-Saudi Arabia, might ultimately create a situation where the Americans could use Afghanistan to put pressure on the Iranian government. It is because of this that Iran is supporting the ousted Rabani government in collaboration with, or at least with the sympathy of, Russia and India.

Similarly, in the case of Central Asia, the issues of trade, transit, oil, and gas have evoked much controversy. Because this was discussed during the lunch break, I will only talk about Iran, Turkmenistan, Pakistan, and Afghanistan. There are different proposals to make oil and gas available to the outside world, either through Iran by a swap system, or through Afghanistan and Pakistan by pipeline. There is a proposal for supply of Iranian oil from Iran to Pakistan, and ultimately to India, through a pipeline. These efforts have run into difficulties, because the American effort is somehow directed toward excluding Iran from arrangements involving the transit of oil or gas from Central Asia.

Any effort to improve the relationship between the U. S. and Iran must involve a gradual process, not a single shot affair, but rather, a step-by-step approach coupled with confidence building measures. Unless it is spread over a long period of time, the process can run into difficulties. A first step could be a resumption of some trade. The private sector could play an important role in reviving the relationship.

Second, there is a need to tone down hostile propaganda, allowing the reduction of tension.

A third issue relates to the initiation of a dialogue which must be issue-oriented; a simultaneous exchange on various issues and matters of mutual interest. Although there may be problems in resolving some issue areas, progress might be achieved in others. Moreover, the dialogue must be aimed at accommodation, not toward proving that the other side is wrong, otherwise the dialogue will not proceed. In response to the question of which should come first, a change in Iranian behavior or the initiation of a dialogue, this could be dealt with by use of a mediator, a third partly acceptable to both.

In the initial stages, the third party could be a go-between, whose role is to pass on the message and to encourage a dialogue. Pakistan has already offered to act in this capacity. In 1971, Pakistan facilitated direct dialogue between the U.S. and China, and perhaps now Pakistan can play a similar role for Iran and the U.S..

"Track Two Diplomacy" can also contribute to reducing tension between Iran and the United States. Unofficial groups, academicians, journalists, and business people from the two countries should start meeting to explore the prospects of improved relations. Today's seminar, in my view, is one useful act of unofficial or "Track Two Diplomacy". Communications of this type can play a very important role. Academicians, journalists, professionals and business people should take the lead over official circles. As they enjoy more freedom than the state functionaries, they can discuss the issues more freely. If the unofficial dialogue improves the environment, the task of the officials will be less formidable. I would conclude by saying that while improved relations between the United States and Iran are of obvious importance to the two countries directly involved, they are also of great significance to the states of the region, because they are feeling the heat of the current antagonism. The regional security environment can improve if the United States and Iran overcome their present-day problems. Thank you.

Turkish-Iranian Relations

Graham Fuller
Senior Political Scientist, RAND Corporation

I have been asked to address the question of Turkish-Iranian relations, which is a very interesting topic. Not surprisingly, Turks and Iranians do not really like each other, but it is not a big deal, as things go in the Middle East. I would say the feeling between the two peoples is not especially strong. There are no deep dislikes, but they each have their stereotypical views of the other. Iranians think the Turks are heavy-handed, slow. Turks tend to think of Iranians as too quick-witted, cheaters, not real men, too much poetry, that kind of thing. But I do not think there is a deep-seated hostility or animosity between the two populations.

Historically, these people have had a great deal to do with each other. The Turks — I say with apologies to my Iranian friends — ran Iran for quite some length of time; at least militarily. Even though the powerful Iranian culture very much incorporated the Turks, the Turks provided Iran with leadership, government and administration for considerable periods of time.

After Shiism came to Iran, towards the end of the 15th century during the Safavid Dynasty, there was a real cold war between the Ottoman Empire, as the home of Sunni Islam, and the newly-zealous Shiites in Safavid Iran. It was a very ugly cold war with nasty ideological exchanges and denunciations by each side.

All this changed very dramatically when Mustafa Kemal Ataturk came to power in the new Turkey, and the Pahlavi Dynasty came to power in the Iranian Dynasty, both of which occurred roughly simultaneously. Most of the past was forgotten; and the two countries began to get along very well. They shared common developmental problems; both of them felt very isolated as each was located between Russia on the one side and the Arab world on the other.

During the Cold War between the U.S. and the Soviet Union, ties were improved between Iran and Turkey, because they were both on the NATO side, on the anti-Soviet side. They both were faced with Arabs on the other side, who, de facto, tended to be closer to the Soviet Union for reasons well known to all.

So there have been periods of considerable ethnic and religious hostility, and there have been periods of great closeness, the modern period seeing much closer involvement than earlier.

With the Iranian Revolution, a new situation arose, because suddenly there was again a kind of Ottoman-Safavid rivalry between the two powers. On one hand there was Turkey, the leading exponent of secularism in the entire Islamic world, having destroyed the Caliphate, and having made itself fully secular. On the other hand, there was a newly resurgent Islamic power right next door that viewed the Turkish experiment as the exact antithesis of everything sought by the Islamic Revolution. So that has been the cause of the rising ideological tensions, even if there have been no ethnic tensions between the two countries.

During the Iran-Iraq War, Turkey was very close to Iran, and was a major trading partner. It traded with both sides, was close to both sides, but the role of Turkey was exceptionally important to Iran. With the Iranian Revolution, though, the Iranians have played a number of games in Turkey. They have supported Islamic radicals off and on, and, on several occasions, the Turkish intelligence services have accused Iran of having backed, if not having been directly responsible for, assassinations of some leading Turkish secularists. The Iranians have also played games diplomatically by taking advantage of Jerusalem Day to have their ambassador speak out, very provocatively, against secularism, right in the heart of Turkey. The last time this happened, a couple of months ago, the ambassador was declared persona non grata, and asked to leave. Also, Iran has been leading much of the anti-Israeli charge within — and very outspokenly — within Turkish politics.

The Kurdish problem has complicated relations with Iran very much. As you know, Kurds are present in Turkey, Iran, and Iraq. The Kurdish population in Iran is one of the largest, second only to that located in Turkey. This makes Iran nervous. If Turkey played its cards right and happened to solve the Kurdish problem to the satisfaction of the Kurds in Turkey —through democratic means, extending them considerable cultural rights and regional rights — it would place great pressure on Iran to do much of the same thing.

And Iran's record towards the Kurds has been poor.

In reference to this whole Mykonos incident, it is hardly news to find a Middle Eastern state killing its own dissidents abroad, yet the Mykonos case seems to be played as something extraordinarily special. Indeed it was very ugly. The killing of dissidents, at home or abroad, is reprehensible, but I find it difficult to view Mykonos as some extraordinary incident, when most other regional states, including Israel, have gunned down political enemies overseas.

On the question, though, of Kurds, the Iranians are very nervous about it, and have, on occasion, supported indirectly PKK incursions over the border, have played games with the PKK in this very complex Iran-Iraq-Turkish interrelationship. Turkey gets very nervous about that particular relationship.

The Iranians have also played minor games in Turkey with the so-called Alevi community. Alevi is the Turkish word for "Alawi" in Arabic, but it is not exactly the same thing. Alevis are quasi-Shiites, and the Iranians sometimes like to suggest that there is some kind of solidarity that should exist between them and Iran. I do not think the Turkish Alevis really believe that they have much solidarity with Iran, but the idea strikes a raw nerve in Turkey because its Alevi population is perhaps upwards of 30 percent of the population. Very real tension exists in relation to this group, and at times this has led to the erruption of real violence in Turkey. Even though it is not prominent on the international scene, the Iranian factor makes Turkey nervous about the Alevi population.

Geopolitically, there is a very interesting tension over Azerbaijan. As you know, Iranian Azerbaijan has more Azeris than Baku does, and they speak Turkish. The case can be made that, perhaps over time, the Iranian Azerbaijanis may begin to feel more Turkish and a little less Iranian, will watch the example of independent Azerbaijan to their north, and try to gain more autonomy at least, and maybe even independence.

In my opinion, deeper problems would be created with Iran's Azeris if the country were dominated by bad governance for a lengthy period. The Turks would profit from the "Turkification" of north Azerbaijan and Iranians would feel that. In a sense, this is a permanent geopolitical gun pointed at the head of Iran. If you talk to Turkish diplomats who have served in Azerbaijan, they will all tell you that all Azerbaijanis consider themselves Turks and seek to be independent. On the other hand, if you talk to Iranians, they will state that they know in their hearts the Azeris are Iranian, are deeply committed to Persian culture and deeply integrated into Persian society. And that is absolutely true, as well. Half the leadership of Iran is probably from Azerbaijan, and doing very well.

Eighteen years after the Iranian Revolution, the Refah Party, Turkey's Islamic Party has emerged. This puts another little spin on the very interesting regional mobile that we see — spinning little balls in the air, all of which shift in different directions when just one of them is touched.

The Refah Party is very interested — as you all know, and as Washington has learned to its discontent — in improving Islamic solidarity in the region. Interestingly enough, Refah could not care less that Iran is Shiite. The Refah Party sees its mission as to resuscitate, to reinvigorate ties with Iran and Iran's role in the world, and to extend its influence on across to Afghanistan, Pakistan, Bangladesh, Malaysia and Indonesia in the creation of a new D-8, the developing eight states.

Now, because Refah is friendly to Iran, because there is a great deal of hostility among the Kemalists in Turkey, and due to the nervousness among the military, the relationship between Iran and Turkey has become particularly powerful and symbolic. It no longer involves just Iranian-Turkish relations. It now includes internal Turkish politics and external foreign policy as well, as Refah consorts and cavorts with various Islamists around the world. This makes the Turkish military and Washington very nervous. So, we are seeing the rise — and I would argue, the permanent rise — of a significant Islamist movement within Turkey; and we will watch Iran's relations with Turkey become an increasingly integral part of Turkey's foreign policy.

The good news is, there is no territorial dispute whatsoever between Turkey and Iran. Those issues were put to rest a very long time ago. Both countries share an interest in Central Asian pipelines as an alternative to the Russia route. Indeed, one would have thought Washington would share the view that it is not desirable to have all pipelines pushing up through Russia. It is in Iran's interest and obviously Turkey's interest — and I would argue, therefore, in the interest of the West — that the two countries be locked into a common pipeline extending through both the Caucasus and Central Asia.

Iran and Turkey both share an interest in having highways running through Central Asia — commercial highways in the full sense of the word — trade, communications, trucking, railroads, all of those things. Both countries share an interest in the on-going independence of the Central Asian Republics and the Caucasian Republics as opposed to their being swallowed up by a resurgent imperialism on the part of Russia, which is still reluctant to let go of the Empire. Iran and Turkey are very much involved and profit from the independence and strength of these groups. They are also rivals in this process.

When officials in Washington sometimes simplistically referred to "Iran, the bad guy, Turkey, the good guy", they overlooked the fact that Iran is actually at a disadvantage in Central Asia because of its Shiism. Turkey is not only pushing the democratic agenda in Central Asia, but is also pushing the Islamist agenda. This is not the policy of the Turkish government, per se, but of private groups — I am not talking about the Refah Party or Erbakan, I am talking about private Turkish Islamist groups that are providing education, newspapers and textbooks, and are proselytizing Islam there, in virtually the same spoken language.

So the Turkish role in Central Asia is as a rival to Iran, but let's remember that it involves an Islamic component, as well. This was underway before Erbakan. So clearly, an interesting tension between the two states emerges, even on the Islamic level.

Turkey is also very nervous about the Syrian-Iranian relationship, as Mr. Melhem spoke about so well earlier. Because both of them see possible support for the PKK emerging from it. Turkey's ace in the hole in this situation is to improve its relations with Israel, which makes not only Syria very nervous, but also Iran, because it potentially brings Israeli fighter planes up to Iran's northern borders. Israeli aircraft could be based out of some Turkish air base, and be able to fly missions right straight into Iran at some point in the future, if such a need should ever arise.

So, real geopolitical tensions exist on the Israeli-Syrian-Turkish-Iranian front. And they probably will not go away very soon.

Let me say a few words about the gas deal between Turkey and Iran. Washington, because of its policies towards Iran, deplores the recent big gas deal between Iran and Turkey. This view is short-sighted, and may benefit Iran. But more importantly, this is very helpful to Turkey. Do we really want Turkey to be completely dependent on natural gas from Russia as it is today? Iranian gas offers Turkey considerable alternatives. Furthermore, if the gas deal leads to an improved relationship between Turkey and Iran, this would, perhaps, enable Turkey to exert a moderating influence in Iran.

The Turkish-Iranian relationship is very complex. I do not think Turkey is threatened by Iran, nor is Iran threatened by Turkey in the sense that we talk about threats elsewhere in the region. Turkey would probably prefer normalized relations with America, and it has no affection for Iran; Turks want to keep Iran under close watch, and at arm's length. However, Turkey would possibly stand to benefit if the tension between the United States and Iran were dissipated.

I do not know where the relationship will go. It is obviously a function, in part, of the U.S. policy in the region. It will remain a very interesting relationship, as Turkey and Iran become powerful players in the Middle East, both of them playing Islamic politics, and both of them increasingly involved in Gulf politics as a whole. Thank you.

QUESTIONS AND ANSWERS

MR. ROSCOE SUDDARTH (Middle East Institute): Would the allies support the U.S.if it undertook a massive attack against Iran?

DR. GEOFFREY KEMP (Nixon Center for Peace and Freedom): I said that the key was Saudi Arabia, and that to launch a really massive attack, you need Saudi support. One concern of the Saudis would be — and Hisham made this point, too — that it would not be a massive attack. It would be a replica of what we did against Iraq last summer, which was not massive and achieved nothing. That is the fear; that we will not have the will or the support to conduct massive operations.

MR. ROSCOE SUDDARTH (Middle East Institute): Is the converse of that true, then, that they would support a non-massive attack?

DR. GEOFFREY KEMP (Nixon Center for Peace and Freedom): I think in the event that the evidence is conclusive, they would be understanding of an American retaliation. I do not think there would be any attempt to punish us or isolate us anywhere. I believe that even the Russians and the Chinese would not do anything. That is quite different from saying they would support us, either before we did it, or physically by providing access, and so on and so forth.

MR. ROSCOE SUDDARTH (Middle East Institute): I would like to ask a general question of all the panelists. Could you just comment upon what your countries would do in the event of a U.S.military attack against Iran, in return for conclusive evidence or semi-conclusive evidence on the al-Khobar incident?

DR. DAVID E. LONG (Middle East Specialist; Retired Foreign Service Officer): The question was, what do our panelists think would be the reactions of the countries which we have been discussing; what do our panelists think about the reaction of those countries if the U.S. were to take military action against Iran in retaliation for its participation in the Al-Khobar raid, given the existence of conclusive evidence that indeed Iran was involved.

MR. HISHAM MELHEM (As-Safir, Al-Qabas, and Radio Monte Carlo): I would still argue that the Arabs, in general, would not like to see a major American attack on Iran. I really do not think this would serve their interest. If the Iranians were involved in Al-Khobar, it would not be the first time a neighboring country violated Saudi sovereignty, nor would it be the first time the Saudis dealt with the issue obliquely, indirectly. At times the Saudis might cajole, might buy influence, or handle things under the table, but not necessarily resort to frontal assault. They might do that in Yemen, but not vis-à-vis Iraq or Iran. I do not think this is their style.

I really believe that they are very concerned about the high American profile in the region, especially after Al-Khobar. Even if the Iranians were involved indirectly, — I am not willing to make that leap yet — it would probably have been executed by dissident Saudis. The Saudi government must deal with this problem, not only in terms of security measures, but politically and economically.

Do you think the people in the EU would like to see their thriving business with Iran threatened by another attack like this? Would the various governments in the region like to see the Iranians lashing out, as would probably happen? Whether the Iranian government gives the orders or not, it is likely that its supporters would lash out on their own. I really do not think the Arabs are aching for an American attack on Iran.

DR. DAVID E. LONG (Middle East Specialist; Retired Foreign Service Officer): Putting on my anti-terrorist hat for a minute, I would like to underscore the point that Dr. Kemp made. These were Saudi dissidents. Even if they were trained and financed by Iran, and if the planning were done in Tehran, the problem would not be solved by military retaliation. I think the Saudis in particular know that the problem is home-grown. They are more interested in addressing the home-grown problem, I think, than in an emotional response.

DR. HASSAN ASKARI RIZVI (Southern East Asia Institute, Columbia University): The states of the region would not like to be in a situation where Iran would be attacked by the U.S.. As far as Pakistan is concerned, I think the government would be very critical of such an action. At the level of the common person, one would see much anti-American sentiment and support for Iran.

DR. GRAHAM FULLER (RAND Corporation): When the question is directed toward Turkey, it must specify which sector within Turkey. Obviously the Erbakan government itself would be very opposed to this. I think the Turkish military, on the whole, would not want to see any such attack come from American bases on Turkish soil, but would probably not mind seeing Iran kept on the defensive, to some degree . . . but not from Turkey, and probably not to an excessive degree.

In general, Turkish public opinion, particularly among intellectuals, is somewhat uncomfortable with America's policing the region, and with the possibility of America's striking back and retaliating unilaterally in the world. This is an action which few other states can undertake.

AUDIENCE: There seems to be a presumption that if a statement is made by an intelligence agency, then that statement is true. Whereas, those of us who have read intelligence reports in the past know that, quite often, this presumption is far from true. I wonder if any of you feel confident or would be willing to provide an evaluation of the Saudi intelligence services and their ability actually to know who was responsible for this bombing.

DR. DAVID E. LONG (Middle East Specialist; Retired Foreign Service Officer): The whole question of who is responsible makes your question difficult to address. Assigning responsibility is a political judgment, not an empirical one. Empirically, one can possibly determine culpability — who did it and who helped. But assigning responsibility, particularly to another country, is a political decision. In this case, it appears that there were both indigenous dissidents and Iranian support. But it is a great leap from support to operational control, and I do not believe that will ever be determined by empirical evidence. Ordering someone to do something he is intent on doing anyway is not operational control.

DR. GRAHAM FULLER (RAND Corporation): I have no particular knowledge about how good the Saudi intelligence services are. I would say that if the Saudis are concerned with a Shiite problem, I think it would be very misleading to think that we are out of the woods. Because really the problem in Saudi Arabia is not with the Shiites at all, who are a small, very much oppressed, unhappy and marginalized element of Saudi society. It is the Sunni opposition which is by far the more fearful. It was not the Shiites, supposedly, who were involved in the Riyadh bombing. Furthermore, the Sunni dissidents now have geared up internationally. Although they are not necessarily all violent, by any means, ultimately the real challenge to the Saudi regime, and the American presence, will be from those Sunni elements. That cannot be blamed on Iran, because the Sunni dissidents hate Iran.

MR. HISHAM MELHEM (As-Safir, Al-Qabas, and Radio Monte Carlo): This is not an apology for Iran, but I think the Iranians know, given what Dr. Fuller said about the Shiite situation in Saudi Arabia, that if they implicate the Shiites in one way or the other, the Shiites of Saudi Arabia will suffer the wrath of a regime that is already oppressive to them. The Iranians know the Shiites can never control Saudi Arabia, so, from a rational perspective, why would they do that? Now, of course, some would say that the Iranians "do not think rationally", and other nonsense.

It is very difficult to find a smoking gun. I spoke with people who were in the U.S. government in 1982 when the Marine bombing of the Embassy occurred in Beirut. I was told it is extremely difficult to come up with a smoking gun.

One of the main reasons why the Saudis do not like for the Americans to have this kind of human intelligence, and to deal directly with Saudi dissidents, is that they do not want the U.S. to realize the extent to which there is dissent in Saudi Arabia. That is it. The Saudis will provide forensic information, lab reports and what-not, but no more. That is all I have to say about why the Saudis are reluctant in particular to allow the Americans to talk to those people.

DR. GEOFFREY KEMP (Nixon Center for Peace and Freedom): I would speculate that there will be no conclusive evidence, for a whole host of reasons. Therefore, the U.S. will not find itself in a position where it has to act decisively. Nevertheless, if the evidence is inconclusive yet circumstantial enough, as indeed was the case in Beirut, it is going to be a dominant influence upon our policy. That was the point that I was trying to get across. For the next year or so, unless there is some breakthrough, this will determine the tone of speech that American officials make. It will determine the way in which this Administration approaches the whole issue of

Gulf security, and the reappraisal of our policies towards both Iran and Iraq. Although such approach may be criticized, any administration would find itself in much the same position. The reality is that on Capitol Hill, the Clinton Administration will experience no diminution of pressure to pursue a very hard line towards Iran. The idea that the offer of better oil deals will enable you to walk through the Congress and repeal the sanctions is simply not feasible, as long as these issues are unresolved, and dominate decision-making in this town.

DR. DAVID E. LONG (Middle East Specialist; Retired Foreign Service Officer): I disagree a bit with Mr. Melhem. During my frequent travels to Saudi Arabia, I have not sensed a seething mountain of discontent there, as was present in Iran before the Revolution. What I think is a more disturbing possibility is demographics in Iran and the Gulf, in fact all over the Third World, where there are population increases of 3.7 percent a year. Populations will double in 20 years. It is a creeping crisis. In view of the potential for political disaffection in the Gulf, security is increasingly going to revolve around demographics, and not around economics and politics. As increasing numbers of people with no jobs are marginalized, this creates a fertile field for political discontent. That is frightening.

AUDIENCE: My question is in regard to the deal signed between Iran and Turkey. We have heard the U.S. State Department state repeatedly that there is not enough information to determine if this deal violates the sanctions. It looks clear to those of us in the room who follow this that the U.S. is not going to sanction Turkey. The question is, will the U.S. inform us that they are not going to sanction Turkey? Or will we to be left in this limbo for the indefinite future? Also, how much do the Turks resent, in your opinion, the U.S.' attempt to stop this deal? They have made it clear that the Iranian gas is the cheapest gas for them, and they really need energy.

DR. GRAHAM FULLER (RAND Corporation): In reply to the first question, I cannot state whether this does or does not violate the intent or the details of the U.S. legislation. In reply to the second question, it is my opinion that there is broad consensus within Turkey, including among those who dislike Refah Party intensely, including the military, that the gas deal is in the Turkish national interest. This consensus is based, not only upon gas prices, but upon the fact that it would give Turkey another source in addition to Russia. Turkey is quite nervous to be dependent upon Russia.

AUDIENCE: If we cross the evidentiary threshold of culpability in terms of this bombing, and we do decide that it is enough for retaliatory measures against Iran, has much thought been given to the proportionality under norms of international law? Are we going to pick out a building with 14 occupants? Or are we going to be a little bit more punitive? Are we going to take an island for a couple of days, and then turn it over? Has any thought been given to the practical elements of this retaliatory message?

DR. GEOFFREY KEMP (Nixon Center for Peace and Freedom): I am not privy to them, but I would imagine there are endless pieces of paper on the subject. The options are almost endless. Clearly at issue here are the costs and benefits to the U.S.. I would distinguish between the need for punishment, as distinct from the need to do something that contributes to the basic long-term goal of American policy, which is to change Iranian behavior.

Of course, there could be a contradiction. Retaliation that is purely punishment, even if it is very severe, may in the short run actually make things worse, because clearly the Iranians have all sorts of capabilities to retaliate. Not against American missiles and warships, perhaps, but certainly against our allies. Iran is not without means, that must be taken into account very seriously. If military force is to be effective in both the short and the long run, then it must be very carefully orchestrated. Clearly, anything that disrupts oil supplies at a time when Americans are getting ready to take off for the summer with cheap gasoline is not something that any administration can ignore.

If the evidence is overwhelming, I would think that the two real options open to the Administration are either to go to the UN to request Security Council sanctions, or to approach the EU, to gain international support.

DR. HOOSHANG AMIRAHMADI Professor, Rutgers University): The time has come to close this conference and thank you, our distinguished speakers and audience, for a very timely, lively, important and productive debate. We will continue our discussions in the near future through additional conferences. In the meantime, let us hope that a new sense of realism will prevail in Tehran and Washington in the near future, and that the two governments will make a genuine effort to build bridges, establish trust, and begin a genuine dialogue for resolving their otherwise negotiable differences. With that hope I thank you again for a spirited meeting.

Speakers' Biographies

Hooshang Amirahmadi is professor of planning and public policy and director of Middle Eastern Studies at Rutgers University. He is also President of American-Iranian Council, Inc., a non-profit research and educational think tank devoted to improving understanding and relations between the U. S. and Iran. In Iran and in the U.S., he has pioneered the public advocacy of building bridges between the two countries. He is a regular guest on CNN, the BBC and Voice of America's Persian broadcasts, among other major media outlets. Professor Amirahmadi has written and edited nine books and monographs, including four on U.S.-Iran relations, and has published over 120 articles on Iran and the Middle East. He is a regular contributor to the Tehran press, where he has published dozens of articles and interviews in Persian on U.S.-Iranian relations, Iranian foreign policy, civil society, and economic development. He is a frequent traveler to Iran, where his advice is sought by the Iranian leaders and non-governmental organizations. He holds a Ph.D. from Cornell University.

Robert S. Deutsch was Director of Northern Gulf Affairs office at the State Department between 1995-97. He previously served as Director of the Bureau of Economic and Business Affairs' Office of Economic Sanctions Policy. He has served in economic and political positions in Italy, France and South Africa, among other countries. His services have included negotiation with the European Community during GATT's Uruguay Round. While serving as Deputy Director for European Affairs, Mr. Deutsch earned the Department's Superior Honor Award. He hold an MBA degree in International Finance from Columbia University Graduate School of Business in New York City and a B.A. in Political Science from the University of Denver.

Graham E. Fuller is Senior Political Scientist at RAND in Washington, DC, where he has worked since 1988 as a specialist in Middle Eastern, former Soviet Union, and Islamic affairs. He received his M.A. and B.A. in Russian and Middle Eastern Studies from Harvard University. He served 20 years in the U.S. Foreign Service, mostly in the Middle East. In 1982 he was appointed the National Intelligence Officer for the Near East and South Asia at the CIA, responsible for long-range intelligence forecasting. In 1986 he was named Vice-Chairman of the National Intelligence Council, with overall responsibility for national level strategic forecasting. Mr. Fuller is a regular contributor to *Foreign Affairs, Foreign Policy, Current History, Orbis*, the *National Interest, Middle East Journal*, the *New York Times*, and the *Washington Post.* He is the author of five books including, *The Center of the Universe: Geopolitics of Iran* (1991 Westview) and *The New Foreign Policy of Turkey: From the Balkans to Western China* (1993 Westview). He speaks Russian, Turkish, Arabic and Chinese.

Stuart Hughes is Counselor (political) at the Canadian Embassy in Washington, where he is responsible for relations with the USA vis-à-vis the Middle East, Africa and much of Latin America. He has held a variety of positions in Ottawa, Mexico, New York and San Francisco. He has also served as Deputy Director of the Middle East Relations Division at the Department of Foreign Affairs and International Trade in Ottawa with responsibility for Canadaís relations with Israel, Egypt, Jordan and with the Palestinian Authority. Mr. Hughes holds a Masters degree in Anthropology from Carleton University in Ottawa. He conducted field research in the Northwest Territories and published a work on ethnic conflict in Canada. He is fluent in French and Spanish.

Geoffrey Kemp is director of Regional Strategic Programs at the Nixon Center for Peace and Freedom. He received his Ph.D. in political science at M.I.T. During the Reagan administration, he was Special Assistant to the President and Senior Director for Near East and South Asia at the National Security Council. He is the author and co-author of several books on the Middle East including, *The Control of the Middle East Arms Race, 1991; Forever Enemies? American Policy and the Islamic Republic of Iran, 1994; Strategic Geography and the Changing Middle East, 1997; and Point of No Return: The Deadly Struggle for Middle East Peace, 1997.*

Michael A. Konarovsky is Counselor for the Middle East, South West and Central Asian affairs at the Russian Embassy in Washington, D.C. He graduated form the Moscow State University, Institute of Asia and Africa, and received his Ph.D. from the Institute of Oriental Studies, Academy of Science, Moscow. He was a Fellow at the Center for International Affairs at Harvard University, during 1991-92. Mr. Konarovsky has held positions in the Near East

Department; Department of Evaluation and Planning; Research Coordination Center; and Department of Analysis, in the Russian Foreign Ministry. His overseas postings have included Kabul and Tehran.

John H. Lichtblau is the Chairman and CEO of Petroleum Industry Research Foundation, Inc. (PIRINC), a not-for-profit research organization. He is a leading international expert on petroleum economics. He has written many articles on petroleum economics and has been a frequent witness at Congressional hearings on energy policy as well as keynote speaker and lecturer at conferences and seminars in the U.S. and abroad. He has served on the National Petroleum Council and is a member of the Council on Foreign Relations. In 1986, he received the International Association for Energy Economics Annual Award for outstanding contribution to the field of energy economics. Mr. Lichtblau is also Chairman of PIRA Energy Group, a private consulting firm.

David E. Long is a Retired Foreign Service Officer of the State Department and a consultant on Middle East and Persian Gulf affairs and counter-terrorism. He served in the U.S. Foreign Service from 1962 to 1993. His Washington assignments included Deputy Director of the State Department's Office of Counter-Terrorism for Regional Policy. Dr. Long has taught as adjunct professor in Johns Hopkins, Georgetown, George Mason and American Universities. His publications include *The Kingdom of Saudi Arabia, The Anatomy of Terrorism, The Hajj Today, and The United States and Saudi Arabia.* He holds a Ph.D. degree in International Relations from the George Washington University.

Hisham Melhem is a leading commentator on Arab and Middle Eastern affairs. He is the Washington-based correspondent for *As-Safir*, the Labanese daily, *Al-Qabas*, the Kuwaiti daily, and Radio Monte Carlo, France. He also hosts a weekly English language current affairs program called *Dateline Washington* for Dubai Television. He is a frequent guest on American news programs such as the *News Hour, Good Morning America, PBS, and Nightline.* Born in Lebanon, Mr. Melhem is a graduate of Villanova University and has lived in the U.S. since 1972.

Bijan Mossavar-Rahmani is Chairman of Mondoil

Corporation. Between 1988 and 1996 he was the President of Apache International Inc. Prior to that he was Assistant Director for International Energy Studies, Energy and Environmental Policy Center, at Harvard University. A former delegate to OPEC Ministerial Conferences, he has published ten books and more than fifty journal articles on international energy markets. His books include *OPEC and the World Oil Outlook, Natural Gas in Western Europe, Energy Security Revisited, and The OPEC Natural Gas Dilemma.* He is a director of Compagnie des Energies Nouvelles de Cote d'Ivoire and is active in industry and international affairs as a member of the Council of the U.S. International Executive Service Corps. He is a graduate of Princeton and Harvard Universities.

Julia Nanay is a Director at the Petroleum Finance Company where she provides clients risk analyses on investments in the oil and gas industry worldwide, particularly regarding the former Soviet Union. Before joining the Petroleum Finance Company, she was a Vice President at the Charter Oil Company, heading that company's Washington office. She also served as executive assistant to the Vice President for International Affairs of Northeast Petroleum Industries, Inc. She received a B.A. from the University of California at Los Angeles and a Masters degree from the Fletcher School of Law and Diplomacy at Tufts University.

Henry Precht was a Foreign Service Officer from 1961 to 1987, with experience in Iran (1972-1976), Egypt, also specializing in Arab-Israeli affairs and political-military issues. He was country director for Iran at the State Department during the Iranian revolution and the hostage crisis. In 1987, following his retirement, he moved to Cleveland, where he served as President of the Council on World Affairs, taught courses at Case Western Reserve University, and wrote Op-Ed articles. He is associated with Search for Common Ground, a non-profit organization dealing with the Middle East. He has a B.A. from Emory University and an M.A. from the Fletcher School of Law and Diplomacy at Tufts University.

Hasan-Askari Rizvi is professor of Pakistan Studies at Columbia University. He holds a Ph.D. in political science and international relations from the University of Pennsylvania. His books include *Pakistan and the Geostrategic Environment (*1993) *and The Military and Politics in Pakistan* (1986).

Nedzib Sacirbey is Ambassador at Large for Bosnia-Herzegovina. His eventful political career began as secretary of Young Muslim Organization of Bosnia-Herzegovina in 1943 for which he served prison terms. He migrated to the United States in 1967, and a decade later became president of the Islamic Society in Washington, DC. Prior to coming to the U.S., he was an assistant professor at University of Sarejevo's Medical School and later served as a lecturer at Cleveland State University. Following the independence of Bosnia-Herzegovina in 1990, he served as the new republic's representative for several important matters at the United Nations, including the country's admission to the world body. Prior to his current position, Ambassador Sacirbey also served as Personal Representative of President Alija Izetbegovic in the U.S.. Ambassador Sacirbey has written widely and lectured at numerous academic and policy institutions and conferences. He is a graduate of University of Zagreb's Medical School.

Gary Sick served on the National Security Council staff under Presidents Ford, Carter, and Reagan. He was the principal White House aide for Iran during the Iranian revolution and the hostage crisis. He is the author of two books on U.S.-Iranian relations. He was a deputy director for international affairs at the Ford Foundation from 1982 to 1987. He has a Ph.D. in political science from Columbia University, where he is currently Senior Research Scholar and an Adjunct Professor of international affairs. He is chairman of the advisory committee of Human Rights Watch/Middle East. He is the executive director of Gulf 2000, an international research project on political, economic, and security developments in the Persian Gulf, being conducted at Columbia University with support from the W. Alton Jones, Rockefeller, and MacArthur Foundations.

Roscoe S. Suddarth is president of the Middle East Institute in Washington, DC. He retired in 1995 from the U.S. Foreign Service with the rank of Career Minister. His posts included Executive Assistant to the Secretary of State for Political Affairs (1979-1981), Deputy Assistant Secretary of State for Near Eastern and South Asian Affairs (1985-1987), U.S. Ambassador to Jordan (1987-1990), and Deputy Inspector General (1991-1994). Ambassador Suddarth attended Yale and Oxford Universities, and MIT. He was a recipient of Presidential Merit Awards in 1986, 1988, and 1991.

Cyrus H. Tahmassebi is president of Energy Trends, Inc. Prior to his current position, Dr. Tahmassebi was the Chief Economist and Director of Market Research for Ashland Inc. Before joining Ashland in 1981, he was a Visiting Fellow at Harvard University. His prior services include senior management positions with the National Iranian Oil Company and the National Iranian Gas Company. Dr. Tahmassebi has written extensively and lectured worldwide on oil and gas topics. He has also served as a member of several important advisory committees on energy matters organized by National Academy of Sciences, the U.S. Congress, and John Hopkins and Harvard Universities. Dr. Tahmassebi holds a Ph.D. degree from Indiana University in Bloomingdale.

Stefan Van-Wersch is the First Secretary at the Netherlands Embassy in Washington, focusing on Near Eastern and African affairs. He joined the Dutch Foreign Service in 1987. At the time of the conference in April 1997, he was representing the EU presidency, a position that the Netherlands held at the time.